IMAGES OF HISTORY

THE OKLAHOMAN COLLECTION

For Andrew and Debbie,

Bob Blackburn

Jim Argo

12/20/05

Acknowledgements

The authors would like to thank several organizations and people for making possible this glimpse into the world of Oklahoma history as illustrated by images from the files of *The Oklahoman.*

First, there would have been no book if not for the inspiration of the Gaylord family and their staff at *The Daily Oklahoman* and *Oklahoma City Times* who recognized the value of the photographs collected for each newspaper. Starting in the 1920s, as professional photographers were hired to gather the images of history in the making, they saved the images and stored them for posterity. Today, *The Oklahoman* archives includes more than a million images of our shared experience.

Second, this book was made possible by the generous support of the Ethics and Excellence in Journalism Foundation, founded by Edith Kinney Gaylord and ably administered by Bill and Bob Ross. This foundation, together with its sister organization, the Inasmuch Foundation, is making a significant difference in the quality of life for all Oklahomans.

Individuals who have contributed their talents to the production of this book include the talented designer, Scott Horton, who quickly recognized the power of the images; Ed Kelley and Sue Hale, journalists who had a vision of what the book could be; Oklahoma Historical Society President Denzil D. Garrison, whose support for the preservation of Oklahoma history over the past forty years has opened new doors for sharing that history; and Mary Phillips, a photo researcher who knows the secrets of *The Oklahoman Collection.*

Others who helped smooth the rough edges of our work include our talented and understanding wives, Debbie Blackburn and Burnis Argo, noted photographer Fred Marvel, historian Dr. Tim Zwink, and outstanding editor, Mary Ann Blochowiak.

Finally, we want to thank our respective employers, the Oklahoma Historical Society and the Oklahoma Publishing Company, for the opportunity of doing what we love most, collecting, preserving, and sharing the stories of Oklahoma and its people.

CONTENTS

Foreword V

Introduction VII

Out of the Earth 9

Riding the Wind 21

A New Frontier 59

Lines in the Sand 107

Coming Together 103

Our Story 175

Original Newspaper Captions 176

Staff Photographers 192

Pioneer photographer William S. Prettyman ventures into Indian Territory in the 1880s.

ington, D. C., before the Interstate commerce commission.

President L. H. Love of the Chickasaw Compress company of Ardmore, I. T., and stockholder of the Pauls Valley Compress company, made two

FRENZIED BY MYSTERIOUS POWER

2 CENT FARE

Oklahoma will have become a state.

At 9 o'clock this morning, central time, 10 o'clock eastern Theodore Roosevelt, president of the United States, will affix

FOREWORD

The photographs you are enjoying come from *The Oklahoman*, which has been riding side saddle with Oklahoma since 1907. The history of the newspaper mirrors that of Oklahoma and of the 20th century. Quite simply, the state and its largest newspaper have grown up together, in a way not unlike that of any family whose love of each other is too strong to succumb to the occasional quarrel.

As the century progressed and Oklahoma grew, so did *The Oklahoman's* photography staff. By the 1930s a staff of seven to eight photographers traveled the state, using the most modern equipment of the time to capture the news of the day. These men who joined the newspaper in the 1930s and 1940s were part of a great generation that weathered a depression and world war. Several of them were in uniform themselves; one of them, George Tapscott, used his photographic skills to record the horrors of the newly opened concentration camps of Europe. Another, Al McLaughlin, spent 60 years at the newspaper; among his many contributions was to introduce color to our pages. These men helped build the modern day photography department of *The Oklahoman*. Much of what they did during their careers and the people they trained to follow them make up the body of work in this book.

As importantly, our collection also includes photographs taken not by news professionals but by ordinary Oklahomans, who thankfully had a shutterbug urge and nose for history that in many instances was just as good as ours. Some of their photos made their way to these pages, and we are grateful to pioneer Oklahoma families who shared them with us.

What criteria should we use to ensure that a relatively tiny number of photos accurately reflect the state's first 100 years? For that we turned to Jim Argo, a former photo editor of *The Oklahoman* who spent 40 years at the newspaper before retirement in 2003. His formula in bringing these pages to life is mostly his own; we trusted him to represent all of us at *The Oklahoman* through this photographic march in time.

Please think of this book as a gift from our family to yours, of a scrapbook that starts at the very beginning but, really, is far from complete. Oklahoma's second century no doubt will be an exciting one, and the youngest among us now will shape the state in ways we cannot begin to imagine. But their path to future greatness was laid by people of the first century, whose hopes and dreams we can feel, we can touch, we can *see*.

Ed Kelley, Editor
The Oklahoman

Staff photographers in the 1930s, left to right, Gerry Allred, Alphia O. Hart, A.Y. Owen, C. J. Kaho and William "Bill" Shroder (facing page).

D MAKES A PROMISE   THOUSANDS WILL CELEBRATE

Oklahoma Governor Robert S. Kerr is photographed by Pfc. Al McLaughlin during a visit to Enid Army Flying School in 1944.

INTRODUCTION

I n the broad sweep of American history, there has never been a story quite like the birth and growth of Oklahoma.

Born as the last refuge for more than 40 Indian tribes, the territory grew as the melting pot of the American melting pot, a last frontier where people from all corners of the world came seeking one more chance, one more opportunity.

This patchwork quilt of settlement patterns retained its vivid colors and contrasts through the early part of the century as the golden age of farming and a series of oil booms fueled the engines of economic vitality. As new waves of immigrants arrived and families harvested the bounty of the land, a spirit of youthful abandon swept across the state as institutions evolved and people learned to work together for the common good.

Increasing mobility, mixed with drought, depression, and the faltering promises of farming and oil, tested the strength of those early pioneers. With each succeeding generation, the historic search for hope and promise changed as conditions swirled in all directions, creating new patterns that blended old colors and textures with those of a new,

emerging world. For some, the result was hard times--others found new opportunity.

War, industrialization, and equal opportunity for all people regardless of race or color stretched the fabric of state history even more. Stories of ambition and struggle, success and failure mixed with lessons learned by former generations who knew all too well the impact of recurring boom and bust cycles. As each experience added another patch to the quilt of history, an image of the state began to emerge, an image as unique as the land itself.

For posterity, it is fortunate that this process of birth, growth, and change occurred during the golden age of photojournalism. At each step of the way, during good times and bad, there was an artist with a camera ready to capture that moment in time. The images that follow, pulled from the files of *The Oklahoman*, offer us a view of that history through the lens of a camera.

Taken together, these images trace the story of Oklahoma.

Bob L. Blackburn Ph.D., Executive Director
Oklahoma Historical Society

Parade in Oklahoma City, early 1900s (above).

After a Visit to the
President, Boom

WILLIAM CROSS

OUT OF THE EARTH

A t high noon on April 22, 1889, everything changed.

For thousands of years, the unplowed prairie along the North Canadian River had been Indian land, belonging to no one person, no one tribe. But the railroads had come, and with that ribbon of steel came a new demand for opening the land to non-Indians.

Farmers who had suffered from the twin plagues of drought and declining prices dreamed of virgin soil and bumper crops, while town builders saw opportunity for profits at every water stop. Congress responded by declaring that the central part of the future state, known as the Unassigned Lands, would be opened as the last frontier – the promised land, the land of milk and honey.

Before the sun set on April 22, 1889, every part and parcel of the territory had been claimed. About half of the 50,000 pioneers claimed 160-acre farms. The others rushed to towns such as Guthrie and Edmond, Norman and Stillwater. More than 10,000 of the '89ers claimed their piece of the promised land along the banks of the North Canadian River in a town that was soon called Oklahoma City.

For the next eighteen years, this transformation was repeated across the future state. Indian claims to the land were extinguished, followed by land runs, lotteries, and allotment of land ownership to individual Indi-

ans. In 1907 the State of Oklahoma was born from this unprecedented patchwork of the frontier process.

Despite the diversity that emerged, there were common threads that bound the statewide community into a tapestry of many colors. It was an age when life moved slowly, confined on a daily basis to horses and buggies. For long distance travel and commerce, the railroads were the only link to the outside world.

Out of the earth came signs of progress. In the rich countryside, orchards, row crops, and livestock displaced prairie, forests, and wildlife. In the towns and cities, one and two story frame buildings gave way to brick structures and skyscrapers rising as high as seven stories.

Rapid change became a way of life, with nickelodeons opening windows to flickering images of another world, while a growing army of automobiles spread from towns and cities to farms and ranches, shrinking the world and creating new bridges between communities.

The result was a blending of two worlds, one the frontier reflections of a bygone century, the other a bustling beginning of a new age. Through it all, Oklahomans raised their families, built their homes, and sought a better life. For better or worse, Oklahoma was growing up.

Despite the common image of the raw frontier, Oklahoma from the 1880s to the 1910s was a blend of town and country. In Oklahoma City, visitors could step off the railroad and find first class accommodations at the Lee Hotel (p. 8) or do business at the Morris Packing Plant in Stockyards City (p. 9). Whether town or country, the lifeblood of the economy was agriculture. In Perry, merchants prospered because farmers marketed their wheat and cotton in town (facing page), while cowboys near El Reno worked herds that had value because they could be shipped to distant markets on the railroads (above).

In an age before movies, radio, or television, people made their own entertainment and created social bonds that would last a lifetime. On a creek near Shawnee (facing page), Reverend L. Walter Nine and Goldie Lutes (seated on the tree) hosted an outing with friends. A young Will Rogers taught Lucille Mulhall trick riding and roping, captured in this photo taken on the Mulhall Ranch in 1901 (left). Lucille is second from the left, while Will is on the far right. Near Leedey in Dewey County (below), the W.A. Foster family proudly posed in their best cloths for this photo in 1902.

A sense of community bound together the people of early Oklahoma. In Pontotoc County (facing page), Scoutmaster T.O. Cullins led his scout troop on a hike from Ada to Oklahoma City in 1909. In rural communities schools and churches became the center of social life for people scattered across the land-scape on farms as small as 40 acres. Above, Congregationalist Minister W.H. Urch posed with his church members (community unknown).

Prior to 1915, horsepower throughout much of Oklahoma literally referred to the number of animals harnessed for their pulling power. J.T. Pemberton, a traveling salesman for Carroll, Brough and Robinson wholesale grocers, reached his customers in his two horsepower buggy (above on left). Robert Galbreath (second from the left in the photo above and to the right) began his career in Oklahoma running a livery stable in Edmond before joining Charles Colcord to build a real estate empire and bring in the discovery well in the Glenpool Oil Field. Pioneers needed animal power to claim land in the land lottery of 1901 (right) and develop their farms (facing page). The farmer is William Harrison Odor, who built the famous "round barn" near Arcadia in 1898.

*Early politics in Oklahoma, from impeachments to unlikely coalitions of
farmers and labor, reflected the youth and diversity of the former twin
territories. Following the removal of the state capital from Guthrie to
Oklahoma City in 1910, the government built the State Capitol two miles
from the heart of the city. Governor Lee Cruce led the groundbreaking
ceremony in 1914 (top), while the grandmaster of the Masonic Lodges
of Oklahoma laid the cornerstone in 1915. Construction continued until
1917, when the first offices moved into the building designed by Layton,
Hicks and Forsythe (facing page).*

RIDING THE WIND

I t was a time of promise, an age of growing pains. From World War I to World War II, life in Oklahoma rushed headlong into a new era of stark contrasts. On one side of the widening chasm were the slow rhythms of rural tradition; on the other were the emerging chords of urban culture. Shaking the worlds of both were the twin engines of boom and bust.

At first, the economy was the wonder of the world. Farmers, blessed with good weather and rising prices, planted more cotton every year, while sodbusters armed with the first generation of tractors pushed the wheat frontier onto the high plains.

Oil pioneers, drawn to the twin territories by early discoveries at Glenpool, spread across the hills of the state where they tapped underground reservoirs of black gold in the Greater Osage, Cushing, the Greater Seminole, and the biggest of them all, the Oklahoma City Field.

As farmers and oilmen harvested wealth from the ground, towns and cities boomed. Oklahoma City was touted as the fastest growing city in the nation, followed closely by Tulsa, the "Oil Capital of the World." Even towns such as Muskogee and Woodward, McAlester and Lawton, had visions of urban greatness as new brick and stone buildings soared above main streets and housing additions spread in all directions.

Then came the hard times.

The Great Depression, which started on the world stage, finally spread to Oklahoma as oil prices fell to ten cents a barrel and cotton was not worth the cost of picking it. Depression was followed by drought. Overproduction followed the increased use of tractors. From the lofty heights of great expectations, the Oklahoma economy of the 1930s dipped to dark shadows of doubt.

Looking for hope, people hit the road. Where once the fireplace had been the touchstone of family and future, the car became the new hearth in an age of increasing mobility and instability. Some found refuge in cities, while others found hope in new government programs such as the Works Progress Administration (WPA), the Public Works Administration (PWA), and the Civilian Conservation Corps (CCC).

Through good times and bad, a personality of the greater community was emerging. The contrasts were still there, as were the divisions that separated whites from blacks, town from country, east from west. But there were shared experiences drawing people together, whether it was reaping the rewards of prosperity or grasping for help in times of need.

Together, the people of Oklahoma were riding the winds of change.

Whether in town or in the countryside, visitors to Oklahoma in the 1920s and 1930s were struck by the physical changes on the landscape. By 1936 the skyline of Oklahoma City (p. 20) peaked at a stage that would remain relatively unchanged for the next thirty years. Much of the physical growth was fueled by the search for and production of oil and gas. In Oklahoma City (p. 21) a young girl on N.E. 17th Street was covered in oil from a blowout, while the search for crude drew teamsters to the Cushing Field (above on the left), to Cromwell (above on the right), and to Seminole (facing page), where mud, men, and round-the-clock drilling transformed a sleepy rural village into a bustling boom town.

By the 1930s rotary drilling and improved recovery methods steadily increased the production of oil and gas, while the Great Depression suppressed demand. Continued drilling in the Greater Oklahoma City Field (facing page), which started with the discovery well drilled by I.T.I.O. near S.E. 59th and Shields (left), led to overproduction and falling prices. Governor William "Alfalfa Bill" Murray called out the National Guard (above) to shut down the fields until oil returned to one dollar a barrel.

Tulsa, 1936.

As wealth flowed from farms and oil fields, optimistic businessmen across the state created a built environment that matched the mood of the times. Tulsa, seen here in 1936 as built by men such as Bill Skelly, Waite Phillips, and Cass Allen Mayo (previous page), had already earned the title as the "Oil Capital of the World." Main Street in Stillwater (above) and the Hotel Aldridge in McAlester (right) reflected that spirit of optimism that the future was full of promise.

The rapidly changing built environment was punctuated by structures that reflected the pace of life and values of the time. In Sulfur (above) businessmen constructed the Belleview Mineral Plunge as a resort for the growing middle class that traveled in affordable automobiles on steadily improving roads. In El Reno (left) citizens raised enough money to build a monument honoring the heroism of native sons who had served their country during World War I.

Rescue workers gathered around the mouth of the Wheatley No. 4 coal mine near McAlester after an explosion in November of 1930 trapped twenty-nine miners below ground. Since 1871, when the mines in the Choctaw Nation were opened, miners had come from West Virginia, Pennsylvania, Wales, Poland, Italy, and Russia seeking steady wages and a better life for their families.

Five miners (left, in the foreground) waited their turn to descend the mine shaft in an attempt to save the lives of their friends and neighbors. Mrs. Irene Nigh, the mother of future Governor George Nigh, and her best friend, H.L. Martin (above), set up a makeshift kitchen to serve the rescue workers. Tragically, the story of the mine disaster ended with a mass burial (top).

By the 1920s and 1930s, the agricultural community was at a crossroads, with many farm families still using the traditional methods of plowing behind a mule in the Panhandle (near left) and threshing with steam engines in Logan County (above). Others adapted tractors to production, as seen here on a farm near Yukon (left), and trucks to getting their produce to market, as seen here in Rush Springs (facing page).

At Crater...

At Craterville Park, Okla.

Despite the destruction of reservations in Oklahoma by 1907, Indian culture survived in the hills and prairies of the state. While Indian communities adapted to changing times in their own ways at their own pace, non-Indian businessmen regularly sought ways to market the traditional dress, dances, and songs of native peoples. At first came Wild West Shows, followed by festivals and fairs. One of the most successful was Craterville Park, located near Lawton, seen here in 1931 (above) with the board of directors of the Oklahoma State Indian Fair Association (right).

Rapid change, both cultural and technological, tested the community's ability to maintain social order. Criminals used the anonymity of urban culture and the mobility of cars and highways to elude traditional methods of city police and county sheriffs. The Oklahoma City Police Department responded with high-speed cars (facing page above), new weapons (facing page below), and strike teams such as the all-Black unit of officers seen here in 1939 (above). The state entered the law enforcement safety net in 1937 when the Legislature created the Oklahoma Highway Patrol (facing page right) with powers to cross local jurisdictions.

The pace of 20th Century life in Oklahoma was revolutionized by improvements in transportation. The traditional mode of cross country trips – railroads – continued to evolve well into the 1930s as the Santa Fe, Rock Island, KATY, Frisco, and other companies improved speed and comfort. With the Firefly steamliner (facing page below), Frisco officials offered a quick and luxurious way to get from Oklahoma City to Kansas City in 1940. Even more radical was the emerging age of aviation. On July 10, 1931, aviation pioneers Wiley Post and Harold Gatty landed the Winnie Mae at the Curtiss-Wright Airport in Oklahoma City after their daring flight around the world (facing page above). For most people, the transportation revolution rolled on the wheels on automobiles and streetcars, as seen here in Guthrie (above).

The outside world came to the people of Oklahoma in the 1920s and 1930s through creative new tools of communication. The motion picture industry delivered a steady stream of images that included favorite son, Will Rogers (above), seen here in the movie "State Fair" with Louise Dresser in 1933. Movie palaces such as the Criterion in Oklahoma City (right and facing page) featured "atmospheric" effects such as Venetian scenery, chilled air, and childcare facilities.

MIGHTY PRODUCTION "DEAD END" with SYLVIA SIDNEY-JOEL MC.CREA
CITING PICTURE OF THE WORLD'S MOST EXCITING CITY

SAMUEL
GOLDWYN'S
PRODUCTION

DEAD END

SYLVIA SIDNEY
JOEL McCREA

LINEN STORE

STATE LINEN SHOP

GIFTS

SYLVIA SID

JOEL MC.C

DEAD END

NO
PARKING
CITY
ORDINANCE

The free flow of news and information also changed with technological breakthroughs. In 1921 the first radio stations in Oklahoma went on the air, eventually offering specialized programming such as "Aunt Susan" on WKY-Radio, which built the first radio kitchen in the nation for Edna Vance, a cooking columnist at The Daily Oklahoman for more than 15 years (facing page). Wire services carried the daily columns of Will Rogers (left above), while newsreel companies captured breaking stories such as the trial of Pretty Boy Floyd in the Oklahoma City Federal Court in 1933 (above). The most popular method of getting the news, however, remained the newspaper. Here, copy editors prepared stories for the afternoon edition of the Oklahoma City Times in 1938 (left).

As Oklahoma emerged from its frontier beginnings, a sense of nostalgia sought to retain the memories of a time that was rapidly vanishing. Oklahoma oilman and governor, E.W. Marland, sponsored a national competition to design and install a tribute to the Pioneer Woman in his hometown of Ponca City. Bryant Baker (facing page) submitted the winning design, which was dedicated in April of 1930 (left and above).

Oklahoma, settled almost overnight by people from all corners of the world, lacked a sense of identity and unity well into the 20th Century. With few shared events to mold a community, many people turned to favorite sons who spanned the divisions between rural and urban, rich and poor. Two of these icons were Wiley Post and Will Rogers, who were tragically killed in an airplane crash in 1935. The mixed grief and love of Oklahomans for these heroes was expressed through memorial services at the State Capitol (above), the funeral of Wiley Post at the First Baptist Church (right) and the dedication of the Will Rogers Memorial in Claremore in 1938 (facing page).

In an effort to relieve unemployment during the Great Depression, the federal government sponsored a number of public programs that also served the broader community. One such project was the construction of a three-mile-long road to the top of Mount Scott in the Wichita Mountains Wildlife Refuge west of Lawton (above and facing page).

For many people in Oklahoma, the economic disaster of the Great Depression was compounded by the environmental disaster of drought and dust storms. The visible impact included eroded farmland, seen here in the western part of Logan County (above), and dramatic dust clouds as seen here rolling over Hooker in the Oklahoma Panhandle in 1935 (right). Efforts to combat the ecological onslaught included terracing, construction of dams, and the planting of trees for windbreaks, as seen here near Mangum (facing page).

Grand Lake Dam under construction, 1938.

Make-work programs and efforts to stimulate the economy during the Great Depression left an enduring legacy that would serve the people of Oklahoma for many years. Under programs promoted by President Franklin D. Roosevelt, seen here touring the Oklahoma City Fairgrounds in 1938 (facing page below right), buildings such as the Municipal Auditorium in Oklahoma City were constructed, while entertainers were employed by the WPA to perform in "Hollywood Cabaret" (facing page below) and in the Oklahoma City Symphony Orchestra (facing page and above). Each building constructed through the make-work programs was marked with a metal plaque (facing page left).

By the beginning of World War II, the skyline of Oklahoma City (pp. 56 and 57) included older structures such as the Colcord, Hales, and Perrine buildings and their taller, newer neighbors such as the Ramsey Tower, First National Bank Building, and the Biltmore Hotel. Until the mid-1960s, this would remain the image of the capital city.

Oklahoma City, 1938.

ports of casualties. No bombs
have fallen in Honolulu it-
self, so far as could be de-
. . . . before this call was

Unverified reports said a . . . . g
. peared off Pearl Harbor and began firing at the
defenses in that highly fortified post.
The sound of cannons firing comes to me here

of the 14th . . . . .
Sunday issued orders short-
ly after announcement. of
the Japanese air attacks in
the Pacific, requesting all
. . . . d men attached

naval stronghold at . . . .
nila were announced Sunday by the White House.
Only this terse announcement came from President Roosevelt im . . . .
. . . . . . be no doubt that the far eastern situa . . . .

A NEW FRONTIER

Nothing would ever be the same.

For much of its adolescence, Oklahoma had been a borderland community defined by contentious politics, exploitation of natural resources, and a cultural pluralism that reflected the rural genesis of a diversified, thinly scattered population. A new frontier was on the horizon.

As had happened so many times through history, the tectonic shift began with the eruption of war. American entrance into World War II wore down the rough edges of a divided community and gave citizens a common cause to rally around. It was a spirit of patriotism, duty, and sacrifice, a belief that everyone had to work shoulder to shoulder for the boys over there.

The war had unexpected results. Military bases, built in Oklahoma to take advantage of location, weather, and work force, created jobs and accelerated the migration from farms to cities. And although the economy recovered from the Great Depression, there were no new cars, no new homes, and few goods to buy. In effect, cash and consumer demand were banked for a better day blessed by victory.

Once the servicemen returned home, they released their own tidal wave of change. College enrollment overflowed capacity, suburban homes spread in all directions, and spending swelled side by side with

inflation. Through it all, the love of country and community survived, expressed through civic and social clubs, expanded government programs, and political candidates who promised reform.

And then came the Baby Boomers.

After years of economic hardship and wartime sacrifice, Oklahomans turned their backs on hard times and started families. Their sons and daughters, born from 1946 to 1964, created a bubble generation with both the numbers and consumer power to set trends and alter the face of the economy. New schools were built, amusement parks, fairs, and zoos expanded to meet demand, and the heart of popular culture, from movies and radio to music and television, beat to the rhythms of the Boomers.

The business community discovered its own frontiers of opportunity. Interstate highways connected cities as the barriers of time and distance broke down, while international companies such as Western Electric and Aero Commander built new plants and retail giants such as John A. Brown and Sears abandoned downtowns to anchor shopping malls in the suburbs.

Whether in the marketplace or in the home, the two decades following World War II were both familiar and uniquely different. Beyond that threshold was a path leading to frontiers not yet encountered.

As America marched to war, Oklahoma's martial spirit was represented proudly by the 45th Infantry Division, which was activated in the spring of 1941. At Camp Barkeley, Texas (p. 58), a battalion of the 45th marched in formal review for the first time wearing gear handed down from World War I. Camp life, which followed a parade through downtown Oklahoma City (facing page), began with morning revelry (above). Oklahoma's wartime Governor was Robert S. Kerr (p. 59), seen with radio stars Edgar Bergen and Charley McCarthy when they played a show at the Municipal Auditorium late in the war.

ports of casualties. No bombs
have fallen in Honolulu it-
self, so far as could be de-
termined before this call was

Unverified reports said a
peared off Pearl Harbor and began firing at the
defenses in that highly fortified post.
The sound of cannons firing comes to me here
this story to the San

of the 11th
Sunday issued orders short-
ly after announcement of
the Japanese air attacks in
the Pacific, requesting all
men attached

naval stronghold at
nila were announced Sunday by the White House.
Only this terse announcement came from President Roosevelt im
it there could be no doubt that the far eastern situa
and that the

Bombs Score
ring After
union 5m
At Honolulu

WASHINGTON Mar
—(/P)—The White House
announced at 3:35 p. m.
(EST) Sunday that the
army had just received

carrier in action against real
The sound of cannonading coming from the direction of
continuing for an hour and a half. So

Unverified reports said a g peared off Pearl Harbor and began firing at the defenses in that highly fortified post.

ports of casualties. No bombs have fallen in Honolulu it- self, so far as could be de-

Sunday issued orders short- ly after announcement of the Japanese air attacks in the Pacific, requesting all

naval stronghold at Pearl nila were announced Sunday by the White House. Only this terse announcement came from President Roosevelt im be no doubt that the far eastern situa

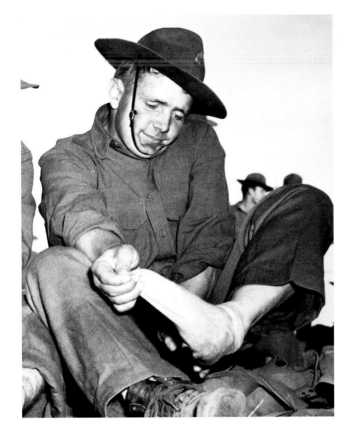

Training for the 45th included camp life on the road to Louisiana for maneuvers (facing page), marching in all weather conditions (above), and a bit of humor provided by Bill Mauldin (upper right), a member of the 45th who created the cartoon characters, Willy and Joe, which later won him the Pulitzer Prize.

As men entered the services following the bombing of Pearl Harbor on December 7, 1941, women filled the ranks on the production lines at the Douglas Bomber plants in Oklahoma City and Tulsa. Lo Dema Davis, formerly a farm wife from Colony, worked on landing gear (left), while other crews modified B-24 bombers at Tinker Field (above) and mixed-teams assembled C-47 cockpit enclosures at the Douglas plant in Oklahoma City (facing page).

ports of casualties. No bombs have fallen in Honolulu it- self, so far as could be de-

Unverified reports said a... peared off Pearl Harbor and began firing at the defenses in that highly fortified post.

The sound of cannons firing comes to me here

of the 14th... Sunday issued orders short- ly after announcement of the Japanese air attacks in the Pacific, requesting all

naval stronghold at Pearl nila were announced Sunday by the White House.

Only this terse announcement came from President Roosevelt im...

there could be no doubt that the far eastern situa...

With scarce resources dedicated to the war effort, Oklahoma families on the home front were expected to "do without" for the sake of the boys on the battle lines. Scrap drives focused patriotic duty on gathering materials for recycling, such as this pile a half block long in Blanchard (facing page), a mountain of tires stored at a local packing plant (above), and a stack of steel gathered at the Lan-man iron foundry in El Reno (left).

Training bases for all three branches of the service were established or expanded in Oklahoma during the early phases of the war. Basic flight training was offered by the Army Air Corps at Vance Air Force Base in Enid (facing page and above). A unit of officers with the, Womens Auxiliary Army Corps (WAAC), arrived in Oklahoma City before being stationed at several towns in the state (right).

Army Air Corps training including flight training at the Muskogee Army Flying School (above) and gunnery practice at Will Rogers Field near Oklahoma City (right).

To prepare for the rigors of war, cadets were pushed through tough basic training (above) and taught skills for survival, such as packing a parachute and safely bailing out and landing on the ground (left).

Medal of Honor winners from Oklahoma included (top row left to right): Leon R. Vance, Jr., Donald J. Gott, James L. Treadwell, and Ernest E. Evans. Also receiving the highest medal for valor were (bottom left to right): Jack C. Montgomery, Manuel Perez, Jr., and John L. Smith. The medal above, awarded to Ruben Rivers, is in the collections of the Oklahoma Historical Society.

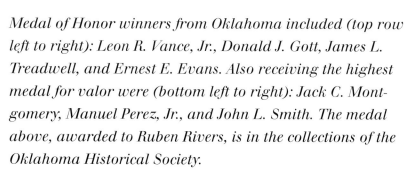

Medal of Honor winner Lieutenant Ernest Childers (above), a member of the 45th Infantry Division, was given a hero's parade in his hometown of Broken Arrow, Oklahoma. One Medal of Honor winner who died in action was Ruben Rivers (above right), whose photograph was held by his brother Robert twenty-three years after his heroic action. Another Medal of Honor winner was John R. Crews (right).

ports of casualties. No bombs have fallen in Honolulu it-self, so far as could be de-

Unverified reports said t peared off Pearl Harbor and began firing at the defenses in that highly fortified post.

The sound of cannons firing comes to me here

Sunday issued orders short-ly after announcement of the Japanese air attacks in the Pacific, requesting all

naval stronghold at nila were announced Sunday by the White House. Only this terse announcement came from President Roosevelt im could be no doubt that the far eastern situa

Members of the 45th Infantry Division stopped for prayer and a formal portrait as they moved through an occupied German village in 1945 (facing page). On August 14, 1945, the people of Oklahoma City rushed into the streets to celebrate VJ Day, Victory over Japan (above).

With the war behind them, Oklahomans reacted to the changing times at different speeds. In small towns such as Hennepin (facing page), life continued much as it had been, a slow pace where the general store also served as a post office. Signs of quicker change were reflected in the new leisure class of boaters on Grand Lake (left) and suburban housing communities such as Del City (above).

The national image of Oklahoma after the war was shaped in large part by athletic teams, especially the dynasties built by Coach Bud Wilkinson at the University of Oklahoma (facing page) and Coach Henry P. Iba at Oklahoma A&M (above), later renamed Oklahoma State University. Another sign of change following World War II was the great play of Sooner football player, Prentice Gautt (facing page left), the first African-American on a sports team at the University of Oklahoma.

anion 5in
BOMDS SCOTE
ring After   At Honolulu

WASHINGTON
—(*P*)—The White House
announced at 3:35 p. m.
(EST) Sunday that the
army had just received
American

carrier in action against Pearl
The sound of cannonading coming from the direction of
been continuing for an hour and a half. So

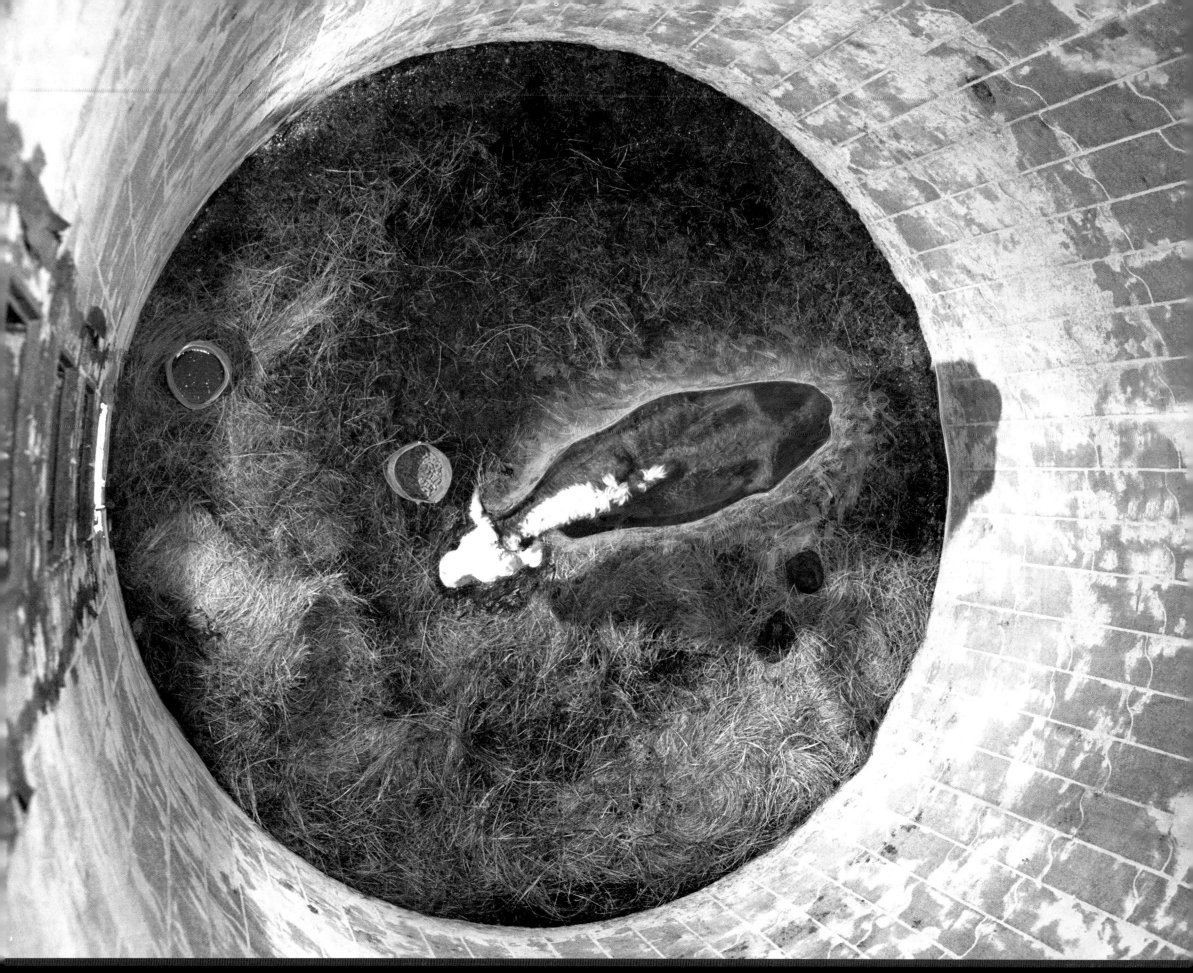

Grady the Cow (facing page and this page) created a national sensation when she was stuck in a grain elevator near Yukon in 1949.

In 1957 the employees at Will Rogers Airport (above) gathered in front of an American Airlines airplane for a group photograph to emphasize the importance of aviation to the local economy. In a failing attempt to revive travel by rail, the Oklahoma Railway Company integrated rubber wheeled busses into their fleet of interurban rail cars in Oklahoma City (facing page above), while Rock Island officials unveiled the Jet Rocket (facing page below), a diesel powered engine that weighed half of the typical train.

Bombs Score
ring After
At Honolulu

WASHINGTON —
—(P)—The White House
announced at 3:35 p. m.
(EST) Sunday that the
army had just received
American

carrier in action against Pearl Harbor
The sound of cannonading coming from the direction of
Hodeer has been continuing for an hour and a half. So

Schools burst at the seams by the early 1950s as Baby Boomers came of age. At Douglass High School (facing page), band teacher W.E. Perry held class for 120 students in a basement corridor. A typical response to the overcrowding was the use of portable "annex" buildings, such as the room seen here at Creston Hills (above). As late as the 1960s, Indian students could attend schools such as Chilocco (left), which attracted students from many tribes across the country.

Lumber Yard

Katy Depot

Ford Agency

A devastating string of tornadoes struck Woodward, Oklahoma, on April 9, 1947. The downtown business district (facing page) lost most of its buildings, while the County Courthouse (above) sustained serious damage. The survivors (both pages) received immediate aid from all parts of the state and nation.

The 45th Infantry Division was one of only two National Guard units in the country reactivated for service in Korea. The returning heroes (facing page and above) were greeted by families left behind.

hair. So far, those ports of casualties. No bombs have fallen in Honolulu itself, so far as could be determined before this call was | Unverified reports said a it peared off Pearl Harbor and began firing at the defenses in that highly fortified post.

The sound of cannons firing comes to me here ... this story to the San | of the 11th Sunday issued orders shortly after announcement of the Japanese air attacks in the Pacific, requesting all officers and men attached | naval stronghold at Pearl nila were announced Sunday by the White House.

Only this terse announcement came from President Roosevelt im ... there could be no doubt that the far eastern situa

After the war, agriculture remained a critical part of the Oklahoma economy. On any given day during the summer of 1951, more than 1,000 trucks loaded with cattle arrived at the Oklahoma City Stockyards (facing page and above). Oklahoma cattlemen often sold more than 10,000 head of cattle on a single day (left).

On May 16, 1953, state officials and the press gathered at the Oklahoma City entry to the Turner Turnpike to cut ribbons opening the 86-mile long "pay as you go" highway between Tulsa and Oklahoma City (facing page). Tollbooth operators (far right) collected the $1.20 fee and gave drivers a ticket stub as a receipt. Before the opening, reporters and photographers received a tour of the highway under construction in 1952 (above and right).

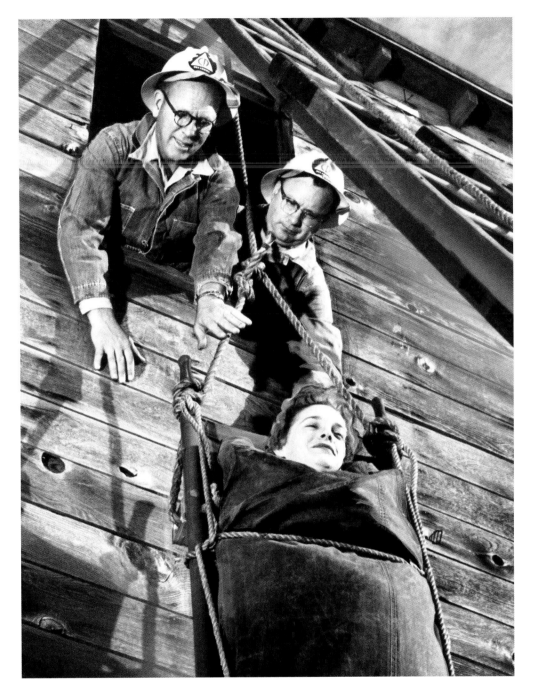

War in Europe and the Pacific was followed by the Cold War, an ever-present state of readiness in the new age of atomic bombs. In Oklahoma, a teacher at Soldier Creek School instructed students how they might cope with disaster (facing page). Civil Defense training, with the ubiquitous green containers filled with water and rations, became an accepted part of life in the nuclear age (left and above).

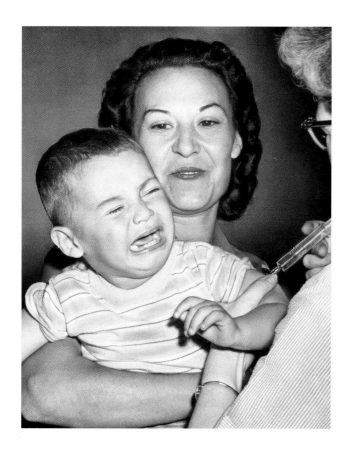

Another survival tactic in the post-war era was vaccination against the scourge of polio. In 1955, more than 7,000 people lined up in front of Northeast High School (facing page), where children reacted with a variety of emotions (above).

Following World War II, Oklahoma City leaders encouraged industrial development to compensate for declines in farming and oil and gas. The new plants included Aero Design and Engineering, which produced the sleek Aero Commander (above and right), and the giant Western Electric facility, where thousands of workers produced switchers and other communication equipment (facing page).

To a generation of Baby Boomers, the Oklahoma City Zoo was a magical place filled with mysterious creatures. Two of the highlights of any visit were Judy the Elephant (above and right) and Monkey Island (facing page), located just inside the old entrance.

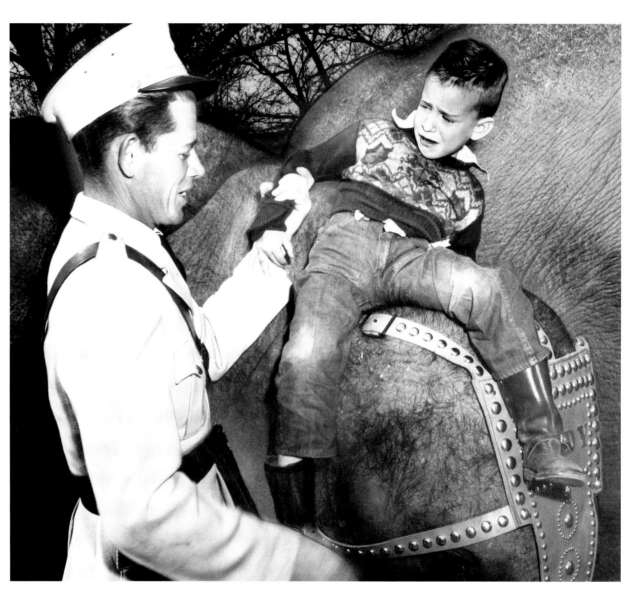

A NEW FRONTIER   101

Bombs Score
At Honolulu

ring After

WASHINGTON
—(P)—The White House
announced at 3:35 p. m.
(EST) Sunday that the
army had just received

carrier in action against Pearl Harbor

The sound of cannonading coming from the direction of

been continuing for an hour and a half. So

Post war families with disposable income created a market for youth oriented entertainment, including Wedgewood Amusement Park (above and far right), drive-in theaters such as the Skyview (right), and Springlake Park (facing page), which started as a dance pavilion and park in the 1920s.

ports of casualties. No bombs have fallen in Honolulu it-self, so far as could be de-

Unverified reports said peared off Pearl Harbor and began firing at the defenses in that highly fortified post.

The sound of cannons firing comes to me here

Sunday issued orders short-ly after announcement of the Japanese air attacks in the Pacific, requesting all

naval stronghold at

nila were announced Sunday by the White House. Only this terse announcement came from President Roosevelt im there could be no doubt that the far eastern situa

Bombs Score
At Honolulu
ring After

WASHINGTON,
—(P)—The White House
announced at 3:35 p. m.
(EST) Sunday that the
army had just received

carrier in action against
The sound of cannonading coming from the direction of
has been continuing for an hour and a half. So

In 1957 the State of Oklahoma celebrated its 50th Semi-Centennial Birthday with an Exposition at the new State Fair Park on West 10th Street in Oklahoma City. Reflecting the changing times, a frontier village (later moved and renamed Frontier City) was contrasted with a thoroughly modern kitchen (facing page) and Teen Town, complete with the latest rock and roll songs and dance that could be heard on KOMA and WKY radio (above).

Thus a s t p o u m d a h
Armstrong, seated in a
landing craft named Eagle
beside his crewmate, Ed-
win Aldrin, began the first

let to hop 2 h
step to the next, said
Coach Armstrong. "It's
very comfortable, you've
got three more steps and

Apollo 11 astronauts Neil Armstrong and
E. Aldrin plant the American flag on the surface of the

a television transmission

He remained out for one hour and 44 minutes.
Their spacecraft Eagle landed on the moon at 3:
p.m., and they were out of it and on the surface som
six hours later.

LINES IN THE SAND

It was an era when walls came tumbling down.

By the 1960s and 1970s, the unity and self-confidence of the war years were giving way to a world increasingly defined by contrast and conflict. Balance—the goal of every community throughout history--was harder than ever to maintain.

This instability was created in large part by the economic and social changes unleashed by the previous generation. There was a powerful centrifugal force exerted by ever expanding suburban housing additions, a new generation of enclosed shopping malls, and the spider's web of super highways encircling and redefining the community.

Even the general economic prosperity of the age, fueled by growing government programs and success in attracting big industry such as Xerox and General Motors, created new tension as people turned from scratching out a living to securing their own place in the sun.

In downtown Oklahoma City the results were startling to a generation comfortable with a skyline frozen in time for more than thirty years. Building after building disappeared, the victim of wrecking balls and urban renewal. As if to emphasize the contrast between old and new, the replacement buildings were citadels of concrete and glass, unfamiliar modern expressions of form and function.

The polarization of the era spread into the streets. Baby boomers nurtured on a sense of individual empowerment demanded immediate and conclusive resolution of their concerns, whether it was the right to vote, equal rights for women, or opposition to the war in Viet Nam.

Young African-Americans, impatient with the slow pace of civil rights victories, stormed the walls of a segregated community.

This volatile mixture of aggressive posturing, public demonstrations, and civil disobedience ignited a powerful counterforce of resistance and distrust that straddled racial, economic, and generational lines. On both sides of the divide, the voice of compromise too often was shouted down by the emotions of violence and contempt.

Through it all, life for most Oklahomans continued to be defined by family, jobs, religion, and entertainment. Beyond the daily images on television, time was filled as usual with decisions on how to cope with gas shortages, whether or not to subscribe to the new television service called cable, or whether to buy the economical VW Bug or the newest muscle car.

Never before had a generation enjoyed such freedoms and means to express themselves in so many ways. Never again would a generation face so many divisive issues in such a short span of years.

eathing again. Thanks a
"Yeah, a three footer,"
Armstrong said.
"Beautiful, beautiful,"
Aldrin added.

day afternoon was hailed
as "man's greatest
achievement," by an Oklahoma City clergyman. His
reaction was echoed by

Methodist Church, agreed
with Mr. Hobbs and added,
"I was amazed that the
landing came off so

off."
"It was a great adventure," Bartlett continued,
"but it is unlike other

beings are capable
when they really set their
minds to something," he
said.

There were humorous moments in the
climbing out and in of the spacecraft. When Aldrin
backed out of the hatch, he said he was "making sure
not to lock it on the way out."

EAGLE (Armstrong):
hank you . . . That may

Armstrong, seated in a
landing craft named Eagle
beside his crewmate, Ed-
win Aldrin, began the first

step to the next, said
Coach Armstrong. "It's
very comfortable, you've
got three more steps and

Apollo 11 astronauts Neil Armstrong
E. Aldrin plant the American flag on the surface of the

a television transmission

He remained out for one hour and 44 minutes.
Their spacecraft Eagle landed on the moon at 3:1
p.m., and they were out of it and on the surface some
six hours later.

As the 1960s began, Oklahoma experienced new tensions that increasingly drew a line in the sand between the past and the future. Downtown Oklahoma City, seen here in 1964 (p. 106), would soon be a battleground of urban design, demolition, and new construction. On the streets, an ongoing vigil against the limitations of segregation was carried on by children and civil rights leaders from 1958 to 1963 (above and facing page). At the University of Oklahoma, students gathered to protest the war in Viet Nam (p. 107).

Per capita, Oklahoma has produced more astronauts than any other state. In an era when heroes were needed, these men and women proved once again that great achievements were possible. Stuart Roosa (above) was a native of Claremore who flew to the moon in 1971. Gordon Cooper (right) was a native of Shawnee selected as one of the original astronauts in 1959. He flew on Mercury 9 and Gemini 5.

William Pogue (upper left) was a native of Okemah who flew on Skylab 4. Owen K. Garriott (lower left) began his career as an astronaut as a civilian scientist. From Enid, he flew on the Space Shuttle in 1983. Shannon Lucid (upper right) was raised in Bethany before joining the space program in 1973. She held the U.S. single mission space flight endurance record on the Space Station Mir. Weatherford native Thomas P. Stafford (above) flew missions on Gemini 6, Gemini 9, Apollo 10, and the Apollo-Soyuz test project in 1975.

Armstrong, seated in a landing craft named Eagle beside his crewmate, Edwin Aldrin, began the first step to the next, said Coach Armstrong. "It's very comfortable, you've got three more steps and Apollo 11 astronauts Neil Armstrong and E. Aldrin plant the American flag on the surface of the a television transmission He remained out for one hour and 44 minutes. Their spacecraft Eagle landed on the moon at 3: p.m., and they were out of it and on the surface som six hours later.

While astronauts defined the hero of the future, Oklahomans continued to celebrate heroes from the past, especially cowboys who represented values such as hard work, toughness, and physical ability. Representatives from each of the western states chose Oklahoma City as the home of the National Cowboy Hall of Fame, later renamed the National Cowboy and Western Heritage Museum. In 1968 (facing page), trustees of the Hall inspected the building under construction. During the 1960s the best modern day cowboys in the world came to Oklahoma City each year to test their skills at the National Finals Rodeo (left). Jim Shoulders (above in center), a native Oklahoman and one of the greatest cowboys of all time, appeared at the National Cowboy Hall of Fame for the premier of the movie "Cowboy," with Jack Lemmon and Glenn Ford. His son, Marvin Shoulders (above left), rode the bull Sonny Boy in 1973.

The largest public works project in Oklahoma history followed World War II when U.S. Senator Robert S. Kerr secured funding for the McClelland-Kerr Navigation system that created a waterway from Tulsa to the oceans of the world. Images from that project include the lock and dam at Webbers Falls (facing page), Lock No. 17 southeast of Wagoner (far left), barges entering Robert S. Kerr Lock and Dam (left), and dedication ceremonies with President Richard M. Nixon (above).

As across the nation, Oklahomans differed over the war in Viet Nam. As early as 1967 (far right), students at Oklahoma State University gathered in front of the Library to protest the war. Three years later (above), protestors demonstrated during an ROTC drill on the Stillwater campus. Others (right) showed their support for the war.

Armstrong, seated in a landing craft named Eagle beside his crewmate, Edwin Aldrin, began the first

step to the next, said Coach Armstrong. "It's very comfortable, you've got three more steps and

Apollo 11 astronauts Neil Armstrong and E. Aldrin plant the American flag on the surface of the

a television transmission

He remained out for one hour and 44 minutes. Their spacecraft Eagle landed on the moon at 3:18 p.m., and they were out of it and on the surface some six hours later.

Anti-war protestors (left) gathered in 1970 at the University of Oklahoma, where an ROTC awards program (top) drew support from both sides of the issue. Highway Patrolmen (above) confronted students who had surrounded a patrol car during a demonstration.

In 1969 an Oklahoma City sanitation workers strike quickly became a protest for civil rights in a community that was still largely segregated. Strike supporters such as Cecil Williams (above left), Clara Luper (above center), and Rev. W.K. Jackson (above right) clashed with police. Angry students from Douglass High School (facing page) marched on City Hall to show their support for the strikers.

eathing again. Thanks a
t.
    "Yeah, a three footer,"
Armstrong said.
    "Beautiful, beautiful,"
Aldrin added.

EAGLE (Armstrong):
hank you . . . That may

day afternoon was hailed
as "man's greatest
achievement," by an Okla-
homa City clergyman. His
reaction was echoed by

Methodist Church, agreed
with Mr. Hobbs and added,
"I was amazed that the
landing came off so
smoothly."
    "It was a great adven-
ture," Bartlett continued,
"but it is unlike other
adventures in that,

beings are capable
when they really set their
minds to something," he
said.
    "We have many prob-

There were humorous moments in the hubbub
climbing out and in of the spacecraft. When Aldrin
backed out of the hatch, he said he was "making sure
not to lock it on the way out."
    on the surface, laughed. "A pretty good

When federal courts mandated that the Oklahoma City Public School System had to be desegregated, the district adopted the Finger Plan and forced busing, which created an angry response through much of the city. Students (above and right) expressed their opinions of the plan, while city councilman John Smith bought and painted a bus (facing page) that could be smashed by angry citizens.

Thus a s... ...
Armstrong, seated in a landing craft named Eagle beside his crewmate, Edwin Aldrin, began the first ... step to the next, said Coach Armstrong. "It's very comfortable, you've got three more steps and ... one." Apollo 11 astronauts Neil Armstrong and ... E. Aldrin plant the American flag on the surface of the ... a television transmission ... He remained out for one hour and 44 minutes. Their spacecraft Eagle landed on the moon at 3:1... p.m., and they were out of it and on the surface som... six hours later.

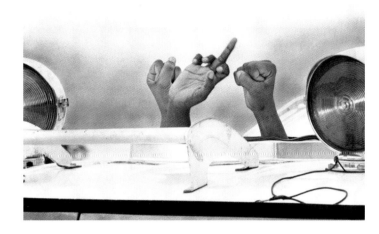

In 1972 efforts to desegregate the Oklahoma City Public Schools erupted in violence at Southeast High School (above and right). Policemen were called in to restore order (facing page).

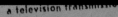

Thus a s . . . .
Armstrong, seated in a
landing craft named Eagle
beside his crewmate, Ed-
win Aldrin, began the first

ler to hop a .
step to the next, said
Coach Armstrong. "It's
very comfortable, you've
got three more steps and

Apollo 11 astronauts Neil Armstrong and . . . . . .
E. Aldrin plant the American flag on the surface of the

a television transmission . . . . . .

. . . . . . Achievement'

He remained out for one hour and 44 minutes.
Their spacecraft Eagle landed on the moon at 3:1 . .
p.m., and they were out of it and on the surface som . .
six hours later.

In July of 1973 inmates at the Oklahoma State Penitentiary at McAlester (above) rioted and destroyed many of the buildings (facing page and right). Policemen and Highway Patrol troopers from across the state (right above) gathered to restore order.

While protests and violence made the nightly news during the early 1970s, most people went about their lives pursuing their own interests. On any given weekend, Oklahomans could be seen in Viking Ships and huge sombrero boats during the Great Raft Race down the Arkansas River near Tulsa (above), at the annual Hugo Bluegrass Festival (right), at the Rush Springs Watermelon Festival (facing page).

Thus a s   'Apollo 11 astronauts Neil Armstrong and   a television transmission fro
Armstrong, seated in a   step to the next, said   E. Aldrin plant the American flag on the surface of the
landing craft named Eagle   Coach Armstrong. "It's   He remained out for one hour and 44 minutes.
beside his crewmate, Ed-   very comfortable, you've   Their spacecraft Eagle landed on the moon at 3:
win Aldrin, began the first got three more steps and   p.m., and they were out of it and on the surface som
         between   long one."   six hours later.

After World War II, the Mike Monroney Federal Aviation Administration Center grew in importance as a site for testing safety and evacuation procedures (facing page, left, far left, and above) and training of air traffic controllers.

Thus a s t r o n a u t
Armstrong, seated in a
landing craft named Eagle
beside his crewmate, Ed-
win Aldrin, began the first

ler to hop
step to the next, said
Coach Armstrong. "It's
very comfortable, you've
got three more steps and

Apollo 11 astronauts Neil Armstrong and
E. Aldrin plant the American flag on the surface of the

a television transmission

He remained out for one hour and 44 minutes.
Their spacecraft Eagle landed on the moon at 3:
p.m., and they were out of it and on the surface som
six hours later.

Urban Renewal, although needed to revitalize a downtown business district suffering from suburban flight, shocked many citizens with the speed and efficiency of the reinvestment program. A daily pastime (far right) was watching the demolition of buildings such as the Midwest Theater (facing page) and the Biltmore Hotel (above).

"I collected money which was turned over to Wal- ters' campaign without being officially designated as a (campaign) subagent," he told Special Judge Rus- sell Hall.

Capitol Bureau

Former Gov. Raymond Gary's life teaches us about moral cour- age and "the need to do what's

ties.

"But above all, I think we should honor Raymond Gary today as we remember him as a teacher," Bor-

the best instincts of our people. And he did that."

Gary, a Democrat and the state's 15th governor, died Saturday of tive heart failure at age 85.

can't believe he said that."

Freeman contended voters were "smart ugh to sort through

ty's funds.

In Oklahoma Coun alone, county comp See FREEMAN, Page

COMING TOGETHER

There was no way to go but up.

By the early 1980s Oklahomans faced many of the same problems that had plagued the young state before. The economy was in a downward spiral following a short lived oil and gas boom that had left the landscape littered with bankrupt dreams.

In Oklahoma City the "spirit of '89" seemed to be fading once again. The population was declining, and those who remained were divided into north side and south side, suburbs and inner-city, rich and poor. The signs of disunity were easy to see, visible in the vacant wastelands downtown, a school system sinking into dysfunction, and a series of public initiatives snubbed by disheartened citizens.

Then came MAPS.

In 1994 the people of Oklahoma City rallied behind a bold bid to become a "major league city." The essence of the Metropolitan Area Projects plan was to invest public funds in a balanced blend of infrastructure, from canals and concert halls to ballparks and horse barns, which would spur private investment and revive hope in a better future. It worked.

Out of the crosscurrents of MAPS, a major investment in the schools called MAPS for Kids, and a rebound in the energy and housing sectors came a renewed sense of community, a belief that what affected one family, one business, one city affected everyone else. The expression of this growing willingness to come together was seen in a golden age of museum development and increased enthusiasm for entertainment venues and sports teams.

That unity was painfully clear to the rest of the world after terrorists bombed the Murrah Building on April 19, 1995, followed by the devastating F5 tornadoes that struck Oklahoma City in May of 1999. The response to those disasters, the unity and compassion for others displayed time and again, established "the Oklahoma standard" of what can be accomplished when people work together.

On Statehood Day, November 16, 2002, the people of Oklahoma turned their attention to the State Capitol to dedicate the Dome, an architectural wonder of stone and steel that was more than a simple building addition, more than the final phase of construction that had begun in 1914.

To many, the Dome was a symbol of coming together, a capstone on a century of phenomenal growth, painful setbacks, and learning to overcome the handicaps of youth. And like the American Indian placed on top, the people of the state could look east toward the rising sun with hope and anticipation of additional chapters to their story.

23, polling site for Freedom... ...d they felt their area of town is glected until somebody wants ...mething.

Oklahoma City Mayor Ron Norick celebrates Tuesday night after voters approved the Metropolitan Area Projects plan. Nearly 54 percent of voters who cast ballots favored the $238 million proposition.

tossed out by a few dozen voters interviewed at various polling locations around the county during Tuesday's vote on a 1-cent sales tax

The second-term mayor was the key force behind work that led to Tuesday's ...osition to finance new

by a five-year, 1-cent sales tax.

The plan passed 32,367 to 27,762 in unofficial returns

In 1982 downtown Oklahoma City (p. 132) showed both promise and disappointment, with vast open spaces still undeveloped next to emerging dreams. With the centennial celebrations of the land runs, Oklahoma's frontier heritage was immortalized in bronze at the National Cowboy and Western Hertiage Museum (p. 133), in Ponca City (above), and in Perry (facing page). Popular interest in the frontier experience was promoted by living history events, such as this reenactor participating in the centennial of the 1889 land run in Guthrie (left).

Oklahoma City Mayor Ron Norick celebrates Tuesday night after voters approved the Metropolitan Area Projects plan. Nearly 54 percent of voters who cast ballots favored the $238 million proposition.

tossed out by a few dozen voters
interviewed at various polling locations around the county during
Tuesday's vote on a 1-cent sales tax

The second-term mayor
was the key force behind
work that led to Tuesday's

by a five-year, 1-cent sales
tax.

The plan passed 32,367 to
27,762 in unofficial returns

As Oklahoma neared the centennial of statehood, communities through-
out the state became increasingly concerned about the preservation of
local heritage, whether it was the music of the Apache played by Doc Tate
Nevaquayah (above), railroad history collected by Bob Read and his son,
Bob, Jr. in Cushing (right), or the reconstruction of the Round Barn in
Arcadia, the realized dream of Luke Robison (facing page).

23, polling site for Precinct is d they felt their area of town is glected until somebody wants mething.

Oklahoma City Mayor Ron Norick celebrates Tuesday night after voters approved the Metropolitan Area Projects plan. Nearly 54 percent of voters who cast ballots favored the $238 million proposition.

tossed out by a few dozen voters interviewed at various polling locations around the county during Tuesday's vote on a 1-cent sales tax

The second-term mayor was the key force behind work that led to Tuesday's proposition to finance new

by a five-year, 1-cent sales tax.

The plan passed 32,367 to 27,762 in unofficial returns

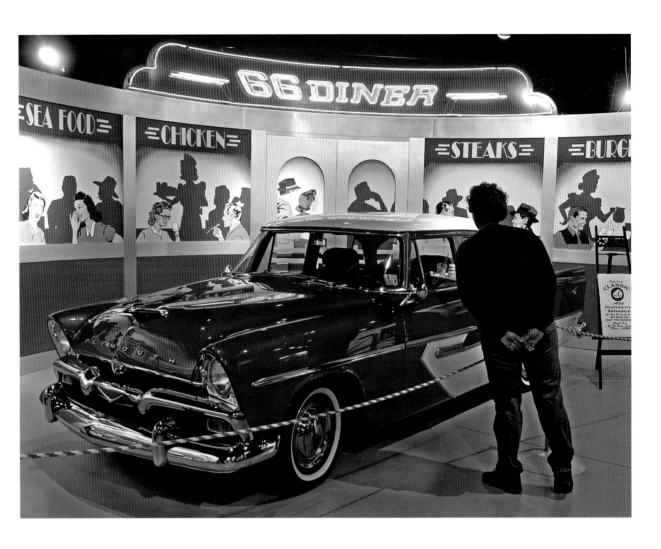

"I collected money which was turned over to Walters' campaign without being officially designated as a (campaign) subagent," he told Special Judge Rus-

Capitol Bureau

er Gov. Raymond Gary's ches us about moral cour- d "the need to do what's

ties.

"But above all, I think we should honor Raymond Gary today as we remember him as a teacher," Bor-

the best instincts of our people And he did that."

Gary, a Democrat and the state's 15th governor, died Saturday of tive heart failure at age 85.

can't believe he said that."

Freeman contended voters were "smart much to sort through

ty's funds.

In Oklahoma Cou alone, county comm See FREEMAN, Page

Cultural preservation and celebration has taken many forms across the state, ranging from popular culture at the Oklahoma Museum of Route 66 in Clinton (facing page, left) and the National Museum of Route 66 in Elk City (facing page, right) to fine art at Philbrook Museum (left) and Gilcrease Museum (above) in Tulsa.

In the 1990s Oklahomans expressed their sense of community through the public and private funding of new museums, including the Oklahoma Aquarium in Jenks (above), the Sam Noble Museum of Natural History in Norman (right), the Oklahoma City Museum of Art (facing page, left), and the Oklahoma History Center (facing page, right), located northeast of the State Capitol.

"I collected money which was turned over to wal- / ters' campaign without being officially designated as / a (campaign) subagent," he told Special Judge Rus- / sell Hall.

Capitol Bureau

Former Gov. Raymond Gary's / life teaches us about moral cour- / age and "the need to do what's

ties.

"But above all, I think we should / honor Raymond Gary today as we / remember him as a teacher," Bor-

the best instincts of our peo- / And he did that."

Gary, a Democrat and the state's / 15th governor, died Saturday of / congestive heart failure at age 85.

can't believe he said / that."

Freeman contended / voters were "smart

ty's funds.

In Oklahoma Court / alone, county comm

See FREEMAN, Page

23, poning site for Fromm...
d they felt their area of town is
glected until somebody wants
mething.

Oklahoma City Mayor Ron Norick celebrates Tuesday night after voters approved the Metropolitan Area Projects plan. Nearly 54 percent of voters who cast ballots favored the $238 million proposition.

tossed out by a few dozen voters
interviewed at various polling locations around the county during
Tuesday's vote on a 1-cent sales tax

The second-term mayor
was the key force behind
work that led to Tuesday's
proposition to finance new

by a five-year, 1-cent sales
tax.

The plan passed 32,367 to
27,762 in unofficial returns

Sporting events, like museums, brought people together, whether it was University of Oklahoma football (above and facing page) or Oklahoma State University basketball (left).

23, polling site for ProbaEl d they felt their area of town is glected until somebody wants nething.

Oklahoma City Mayor Ron Norick celebrates Tuesday night after voters approved the Metropolitan Area Projects plan. Nearly 54 percent of voters who cast ballots favored the $238 million proposition.

tossed out by a few dozen voters interviewed at various polling locations around the county during Tuesday's vote on a 1-cent sales tax

The second-term mayor was the key force behind work that led to Tuesday's proposition to finance new

by a five-year, 1-cent sales tax.

The plan passed 32,367 to 27,762 in unofficial returns

"I collected money which was turned over to war-
ters' campaign without being officially designated as
a (campaign) subagent," he told Special Judge Russell Hall.

Capitol Bureau

Former Gov. Raymond Gary's
life teaches us about moral courage and "the need to do what's

Democrat
ties.

"But above all, I think we should
honor Raymond Gary today as we
remember him as a teacher," Bor-

the best instincts of our people.
And he did that."

Gary, a Democrat and the state's
15th governor, died Saturday of
heart failure at age 85.

can't believe he said
that."

Freeman contended
voters were "smart

ty's funds.

In Oklahoma Coun-
alone, county comm
See **FREEMAN**, Page

On April 19, 1995, a truck bomb changed the course of history in an instant. That morning of terror reduced the Murrah Building to ruins (facing page), took the lives of 168 people, and injured hundreds more (left and above).

Rescue efforts after the bombing of the Murrah Building drew on the courage of local firemen and policemen as well as volunteers from across the country (facing page). One rescue worker placed flowers on the site (left), while news of the rescue effort were beamed to the rest of the world by a small army of broadcasters (above, top). Within days, President Bill Clinton and Governor Frank Keating joined family members of victims and survivors in a memorial service (above).

"I collected money which was turned over to Walters' campaign without being officially designated as a (campaign) subagent," he told Special Judge Rus-

Capitol Bureau

Former Gov. Raymond Gary's life teaches us about moral courage and "the need to do what's

"But above all, I think we should honor Raymond Gary today as we remember him as a teacher," Bor-

the best instincts of our people. And he did that."

Gary, a Democrat and the state's 15th governor, died Saturday of heart failure at age 85.

can't believe he said that."

Freeman contended voters were "smart

ty's funds.

In Oklahoma County alone, county comm See FREEMAN, Page

Grief, whether it was for lost family and friends or simply the feeling of tragic loss, was expressed by thousands of people who left mementoes on the chain link fence surrounding the bombing site (facing page). Survivors (left) watched as the ruins of the Murrah Building were demolished (above).

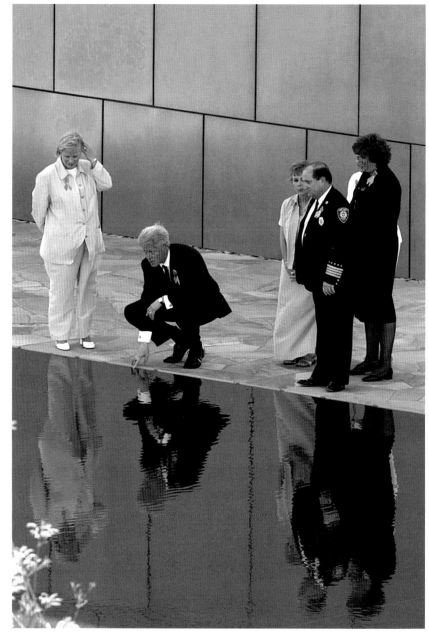

"I collected money which was turned over to Walters' campaign without being officially designated as
a (campaign) subagent," he told Special Judge Russell Hall.

Capitol Bureau

Former Gov. Raymond Gary's
life teaches us about moral courage and "the need to do what's

ties.

"But above all, I think we should
honor Raymond Gary today as we
remember him as a teacher," Bor-

the best instincts of our people.
And he did that."

Gary, a Democrat and the state's
15th governor, died Saturday of
congestive heart failure at age 85.

can't believe he said
that."

Freeman contended
voters were "smart
enough to sort through

ty's funds.

In Oklahoma Court
alone, county comm
See FREEMAN, Page

To memorialize the lives lost and changed forever, the site of the bombing became a place for reflection and contemplation. The Survivors' Tree (facing page, left), located between the Murrah Building and the Journal Record Building, became a symbol of resilience. Presidents Clinton (facing page, right) and Bush (above), returned to show their respects. Family members of victims (left and far left) returned to deal with their sense of loss.

After a century of immigration and assimilation, the spirit of diversity in Oklahoma was expressed in a variety of ways. Clara Luper (above seated on bench), a pioneer in the sit-in movement of the early 1960s, spoke to a group at the Oklahoma Historical Society on Martin Luther King Day. A young Sac and Fox girl (right) gathered with family and friends at a Powwow near Stroud. In Oklahoma City, families from Viet Nam (facing page, left), Korea (facing page, center), and Mexico (facing page, right) preserved traditions from their homelands through festivals and ceremonies.

The first project to be completed as part of MAPS (Metropolitan Area Projects) was the Bricktown Ball Park (facing page and right). Located at the home plate entrance was a monumental statue of Mickey Mantle (above), a native Oklahoman who starred with the New York Yankees.

Key to the success of MAPS was the effort to bring people together, whether it was on the Bricktown Canal (facing page), a performance on the Civic Center stage (left), or water sports on the North Canadian River (above).

| | Capitol Bureau | | the best instincts of our people. | can't believe he said | ty's funds. |

"I collected money which was turned over to Walters' campaign without being officially designated as
a (campaign) subagent," he told Special Judge Russell Hall.

Former Gov. Raymond Gary's
life teaches us about moral courage and "the need to do what's

Democrats-
ties.

"But above all, I think we should
honor Raymond Gary today as we
remember him as a teacher," Bor-

And he did that."

Gary, a Democrat and the state's
15th governor, died Saturday of
a heart failure at age 85

that."

Freeman contended
voters were "smart

In Oklahoma Coun-
alone, county comm
See **FREEMAN**, Page

The last of the MAPS projects to be completed were the Ford Arena (facing page), seen here when the Circus became the first performance after the grand opening, and the Ronald J. Norick Downtown Library (above), named in honor of the mayor who championed the MAPS cause.

"I collected money which was turned over to Walters' campaign without being officially designated as
a (campaign) subagent," he told Special Judge Russell Hall.

Capitol Bureau

Former Gov. Raymond Gary's
life teaches us about moral courage and "the need to do what's

ties.

"But above all, I think we should
honor Raymond Gary today as we
remember him as a teacher," Bor-

the best instincts of our people.
And he did that."

Gary, a Democrat and the state's
15th governor, died Saturday of
congestive heart failure at age 85.

can't believe he said
that."

Freeman contended
voters were "smart

ty's funds.

In Oklahoma Cou
alone, county comm
See **FREEMAN**, Page

On May 3, 1999, a deadly F5 tornado (facing page) was captured in this photograph as it passed over Pennsylvania Avenue at S.W. 134th Street. Rescue workers moved in quickly to help victims (above left) and search for survivors (above right).

More than half of the 15,000 homes in Moore suffered tornado damage, including this swath of devastation near Interstate 35 (facing page). Survivors (far left, left, and above) reacted with faith, action, and despair.

Military bases established in Oklahoma during World War II continued to serve the Armed Services during Korea, Viet Nam, the Cold War, Desert Storm, and Iraq while contributing to the economic strength of local communities. A crew on a KC-135 Stratotanker from Altus Air Force Base (above) refueled a jet in flight. An E-3A from the 552nd Air Control Wing at Tinker Air Force Base (facing page) served as a backdrop for a change of command ceremony.

"I collected money which was turned over to war- ters' campaign without being officially designated as a (campaign) subagent," he told Special Judge Rus- sell Hall.

Capitol Bureau

Former Gov. Raymond Gary's life teaches us about moral cour- age and "the need to do what's

ties.

"But above all, I think we should honor Raymond Gary today as we remember him as a teacher," Bor-

the best instincts of our people. And he did that."

Gary, a Democrat and the state's 15th governor, died Saturday of

can't believe he said that."

Freeman contended voters were "smart

ty's funds.

In Oklahoma Court alone, county comm See **FREEMAN**, Page

Oklahoma City Mayor Ron Norick celebrates Tuesday night after voters approved the Metropolitan Area Projects plan. Nearly 54 percent of voters who cast ballots favored the $238 million proposition.

tossed out by a few dozen voters
interviewed at various polling locations around the county during
Tuesday's vote on a 1-cent sales tax

The second-term mayor
was the key force behind
work that led to Tuesday's
proposition to finance new

by a five-year, 1-cent sales
tax.

The plan passed 32,367 to
27,762 in unofficial returns

For more than 100 years, Oklahoma has been a source of energy for the country and world, creating jobs, generating tax revenues, and building a capital base for further investments. The search for oil and gas now regularly takes drillers more than two miles below the surface (facing page), while wind turbines generate electricity in fields across western Oklahoma (above and left).

Wheat and cotton may still dominate Oklahoma farm acreage, but urbanization, new marketing tools, and mechanization have encouraged land owners to try specialized agriculture such as Christmas tree farms (above), vineyards and wineries (right), and pecans (facing page).

Oklahoma City Mayor Ron Norick celebrates Tuesday night after voters approved the Metropolitan Area Projects plan. Nearly 54 percent of voters who cast ballots favored the $238 million proposition.

tossed out by a few dozen voters interviewed at various polling locations around the county during Tuesday's vote on a 1-cent sales tax

The second-term mayor was the key force behind work that led to Tuesday's proposition to finance new

by a five-year, 1-cent sales tax.

The plan passed 32,367 to 27,762 in unofficial returns

Construction of the dome, accomplished through a combination of public and private financing, involved the public in the process of completing the State Capitol, the symbol of a unified state. Visitors signed their names to the main support beams (above and right), while State Senator Enoch Kelly Haney put the finishing touches on the Guardian (facing page, left), which was placed on top of the dome. A construction supervisor with the Manhattan-Flintco team inspected the base of the new dome (facing page, right).

E 23, polling site for Precinct
id they felt their area of town is
eglected until somebody wants
mething.

**Oklahoma City Mayor Ron Norick celebrates Tuesday night after voters
approved the Metropolitan Area Projects plan. Nearly 54 percent of voters
who cast ballots favored the $238 million proposition.**

tossed out by a few dozen voters
interviewed at various polling locations around the county during
Tuesday's vote on a 1-cent sales tax

The second-term mayor
was the key force behind
work that led to Tuesday's
proposition to finance new

by a five-year, 1-cent sales
tax.

The plan passed 32,367 to
27,762 in unofficial returns

Ice.

"I collected money which was turned over to Walters' campaign without being officially designated as a (campaign) subagent," he told Special Judge Russell Hall.

Capitol Bureau

Former Gov. Raymond Gary's life teaches us about moral courage and "the need to do what's

ties.

"But above all, I think we should honor Raymond Gary today as we remember him as a teacher," Bor-

the best instincts of our people. And he did that."

Gary, a Democrat and the state's 15th governor, died Saturday of ative heart failure at age 85.

can't believe he said that."

Freeman contended voters were "smart

ty's funds.

In Oklahoma County alone, county comm See **FREEMAN**, Page

Ceremonies to dedicate the completed dome included fireworks (facing page), singers Leona Mitchell (far left), Vince Gill (left), and three Miss Americas from Oklahoma, Shawntel Smith-Wuerch, Jane Jayroe, and Susan Powell. (above, left to right).

"I collected money which was turned over to war-
ters' campaign without being officially designated as
a (campaign) subagent," he told Special Judge Russell Hall

Capitol Bureau

Former Gov. Raymond Gary's
life teaches us about moral courage and "the need to do what's

ties.

"But above all, I think we should
honor Raymond Gary today as we
remember him as a teacher," Bor-

the best instincts of our people.
And he did that."

Gary, a Democrat and the state's
15th governor, died Saturday of
native heart failure at age 85.

can't believe he said
that."

Freeman contended
voters were "smart
enough to sort through

ty's funds.

In Oklahoma Coun
alone, county comm
See **FREEMAN**, Page

OUR STORY

For the past 100 years, the story of Oklahoma has been unfolding, one page at a time, one chapter following another. What have we learned?

As in our individual lives, we know that stability and wisdom come with age and experience. Youth, although full of energy and the heady brew of future possibilities, often comes at the cost of mistakes, missed opportunities, and sometimes failure. In the early story of Oklahoma, that trail of misfortune is strewn with impeachments, exploitation of Indian lands, and bitter rivalries that often held everyone back.

At the same time, youth comes with big dreams, faith in the future, and a spirit that sees few boundaries. That youthful vigor encouraged oilmen to invest every penny in the next well, merchants to find innovative ways to sell for less, and farmers to plant one more field in hopes of reaping the bumper crop of their dreams.

We also know that diversity has two sides, one providing character and depth, the other fostering mistrust and disunity. For Oklahomans throughout much of the 20th Century, public life was fractured along the lines between old Oklahoma Territory and old Indian Territory, the business community against the farmer-labor coalition, and people of color against the white majority.

Yet today, we treasure the Indian elder who remembers the songs of his ancestors. We celebrate the perseverance of pioneer families who still prepare the foods of their native lands. And we promote the variety of destinations for tourists who are looking for something new, something unique that sheds light on who we are. The path from the former to the latter, in many ways, leads to a better understanding of our progress as a state.

Then there are the people.

History, which after all is our story, is best understood through the cumulative impact and experience of individual men and women who have raised their families, earned a living, and practiced their faith on the land we call Oklahoma.

We are the Indian leaders who held off the advancing American frontier so our people had time to adjust to a new world. We are the farmers who broke the sod and planted the crops so our children could get an education. And we are the immigrants who came to Oklahoma for freedom and a future full of hope.

Our history, as captured by the photojournalists at *The Oklahoman*, is all of this and more. It is the Oklahoma experience.

ORIGINAL NEWSPAPER CAPTIONS

Alvin Rucker was a photographer/reporter who traveled throughout Oklahoma doing stories and an occasional photo for *The Daily Oklahoman* and the *Oklahoma City Times*. Rucker joined *The Daily Oklahoman* in 1912 and for the next 22 years traveled the state from Black Mesa in the Panhandle to the Mountain Fork River in McCurtain County, long before roadways were paved. He was primarily a reporter but also served as the first staff photographer for both newspapers.

On a cold and windy December morning, Rucker and a reporter for the afternoon *Oklahoma City Times* were watching as oil field workers were preparing to bring in the first well to be drilled in Oklahoma City. Suddenly the well erupted, spewing black oil. Rucker jumped out of his press car and in his own words, "I snapped five pictures and ran back to the car, and drove rapidly as possible to the Oklahoman building."

The next day, December 5, 1928, *The Daily Oklahoman* published on page one this photograph of the I.T.I.O (Indian Territory Illuminating Oil and Foster Petroleum companies) well as oil gushed forth. The afternoon *Oklahoma City Times* published the same photo full page, only for some unknown reason reversed the photo, adding the headline:

Oklahoma City's First Gusher! and a small graphics box. Rucker was given photo credit in both papers for this historic picture, a rarity in those days.

Through the years, the newspaper has conducted photo contests seeking "early day" photos of pioneer families and events, always requesting full information including names, dates, places, and event titles. Often these photographs would be used in special editions of the paper and winners were rewarded with a small cash prize.

Many photographs in *The Oklahoman Collection* have come from early day professional studio photographers and are being published for the first time. By the 1930s both *The Daily Oklahoman* and its sister publication, the *Oklahoma City Times*, had full-time staff photographers.

The original captions, as they appeared in the newspapers in which they were published, have been copied for use in this book, even though the style and punctuation used in past years does not necessarily meet today's newspaper style.

Compiled by Jim Argo
Researched by Mary Phillips

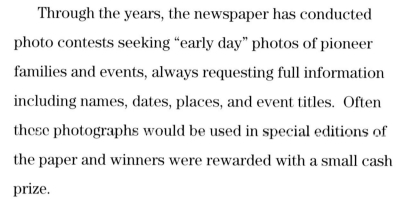

FRONT MATTER

Page III (Contents)

Pioneer photographer William S. Prettyman ventures into Indian Territory in the 1880s. Prettyman later opened a studio in Arkansas City, Kan. He became famous when he constructed a tall platform and stationed two photographers to photograph the historic Cherokee Land Run of 1893. Prettyman participated in the run, staking his claim in present day Blackwell. Photo courtesy of The Glass Negative/*THE OKLAHOMAN COLLECTION*. Published April 22, 1989, *THE SUNDAY OKLAHOMAN*.

Page 4 (Foreword)

The first five photographers for *The Daily Oklahoman* and the afternoon paper, the *Oklahoma City Times*, strike a formal pose with their 1930's cameras. Left to right, Gerry Allred, Alphia O. Hart, A.Y. Owen, C.J. Kaho and William "Bill" Shroder, Jr. Staff Photo. *THE OKLAHOMAN COLLECTION*. Jan. 21, 1937. Unpublished.

Page 6 (Introduction)

Pfc. Al McLaughlin photographs a visit to Vance Air Force Base, Enid, Okla., by Governor Robert S. Kerr. McLaughlin, a former photographer for *The Daily Oklahoman* and *Oklahoma City Times*, enlisted in the military during World War II. *THE OKLAHOMAN COLLECTION*. Nov. 21, 1944. Unpublished.

CHAPTER ONE
OUT OF THE EARTH

Page 8

The Lee was the main hotel until it burned in August, 1908. It was sold to the Huckins interests a few years before and was known as the Lee-Huckins. It was rebuilt immediately as the present day Huckins at Main Street and Broadway. *THE OKLAHOMAN COLLECTION*. Published Mar. 1, 1953, *THE DAILY OKLAHOMAN*.

Page 9

High button shoes, fancy shirtwaists—and hats—were standard wearing apparel only 40 years ago, as this "picture" surely proves. It was made in 1910 on the steps of the office building of what was then the Morris packing plant. It was the forerunner of the present-day Armour & Co. plant in the stockyards area and gave Oklahoma City a powerful industrial push in those days. This third prize winner in the single picture class was submitted by Mrs. T.H. Benhoff. *THE OKLAHOMAN COLLECTION*. Published Apr. 23, 1950, *THE DAILY OKLAHOMAN*.

Page 10

This picture of the E.J. Miller grain elevator taken July 7, 1902, in Perry, illustrates the agricultural roots that remained a dominant part of rural Oklahoma life through much of the state's history. Photo submitted by Mary Katherine Miller, Midwest City. *THE OKLAHOMAN COLLECTION*. Published Nov. 15, 1987, *THE SUNDAY OKLAHOMAN*.

Page 11

Rounding up cattle trespassing on the Military reservation around Ft. Reno-1901. *THE OKLAHOMAN COLLECTION*. Unpublished.

Page 12

The distinguished looking man sitting on the log with the girl just in front of him is the Rev. L. Walter Nine. Seated in front of him is Miss Goldie Lutes, then his fiancee, later his wife. She's the one who teaches in a school for the blind at Kansas City, Kan. The woman standing is Mrs. Mattie Crampton and the old man sitting on the log is John Lutes, on a creek near Shawnee. *THE OKLAHOMAN COLLECTION*. Unpublished.

Page 13 (top)

HE TAUGHT HER — "It the most terrible thing that ever happened to me," choked Lucille Mulhall, famed cowgirl, at the news of the tragic death of Will Rogers. He was the young cowboy who taught 16-year-old Lucille trick roping and riding that gave her world fame as "the first cowgirl." Rogers is shown at the extreme right with members of the Mulhall troupe, who gave the world "rodeo's" at the turn of the century. Others left to right are Agnes Mulhall, Lucille Mulhall and a puncher remembered only as "Shorty." The picture was made at the Mulhall ranch in 1901; was given to L.W. Hicks, by Agnes Mulhall, while the troupe was at the St. Louis world's fair. *THE OKLAHOMAN COLLECTION*. Published Aug. 17, 1935, *THE DAILY OKLAHOMAN*.

Page 13 (bottom)

W. A. Foster and family members in front of a dugout, Leedey, Dewey Co., Oklahoma Territory, June 10, 1902. *THE OKLAHOMAN COLLECTION*. Unpublished

Page 14

Photo was made in 1909 when T.O. Cullins, Ada, was scout master of the first boy scout troop in Pontotoc County. The troop hiked to Oklahoma City and were the guests of a local scout troop. The Ada scouts returned home on a special MKT train coach. *THE OKLAHOMAN COLLECTION*. Unpublished.

Page 15

An early day Congregationalist minister was Dr. W.H. Urch, left, an Englishman who came as a missionary to the United States. He was a scholarly, dignified man who remained interested in missionary work. *THE OKLAHOMAN COLLECTION*. Unpublished.

Page 16 (top left)

This is the way salesmen "covered" their territory before the days of speedometers and mileage allowances. J.T. Pemberton, in the buggy, is one of Oklahoma's "veterans of the grip." He was the first salesman for Carroll & Brough, remained with the enlarged firm of Carroll, Brough & Robinson, wholesale grocers. With him was Charles Wheeler, hardware salesman. *THE OKLAHOMAN COLLECTION*. Unpublished.

Page 16 (top right)

Robert Galbreath, second from left, and his livery stable in Edmond in the 1890's. *THE OKLAHOMAN COLLECTION*. Published Mar. 24, 1934, *OKLAHOMA CITY TIMES*.

Page 16 (bottom)

Early day settlers in wagon trains move through tent city (in Lawton) before the lottery of 1901. *THE OKLAHOMAN COLLECTION*. Unpublished.

Page 17

Horse drawn wagons in front of the Arcadia round barn built 1898, by William Harrison Odor. The two-story barn is 43 feet high and 60 feet in diameter. It was used to store hay, grain and livestock. *THE OKLAHOMAN COLLECTION*. Published Apr. 16, 1989, *THE SUNDAY OKLAHOMAN*.

Page 18 (top left)

Gov. Lee Cruce officiates at a festive groundbreaking for the Capitol in July 1914. *THE OKLAHOMAN COLLECTION*. Published Apr. 16, 1989, *THE SUNDAY OKLAHOMAN*.

Page 18 (bottom left)

The Tishomingo granite cornerstone of the Oklahoma Capitol building was laid Nov. 16, 1915, the eighth anniversary of Statehood Day, by the late Almer E. Monroney, grandmaster of the Masonic Lodges of Oklahoma, as more than 15,000 persons watched. Monroney, father of Sen. Mike Monroney, and Mrs. Frank Harbinson used a silver trowel in the ceremony. *THE OKLAHOMAN COLLECTION*. Published Nov. 10, 1957, *THE SUNDAY OKLAHOMAN*.

Page 19

The construction of the Oklahoma State Capitol building was well underway when this picture was taken Nov. 15, 1916. *THE OKLAHOMAN COLLECTION.* Published Nov. 10, 1957, *THE SUNDAY OKLAHOMAN.*

CHAPTER TWO
RIDING THE WIND

Page 20

The busy southwest corner of Main and Robinson in Oklahoma City, as it appeared in 1936. *THE OKLAHOMAN COLLECTION.* Unpublished.

Page 21

Though she felt sticky and slick, Imogene Maxine Holden, 8 years old, who was playing in her yard, could still grin about it. (She was covered in oil). *THE OKLAHOMAN COLLECTION.* Published July 21, 1936, *THE DAILY OKLAHOMAN.*

Page 22 (left)

It took some doing to haul oil field equipment around in the boom days of the Cushing field. Equipment then was not as heavy as it is now, but it was tough enough. Here a six-team hitch drags a boiler across a ford in the Cimarron river. (Photo Undated) *THE OKLAHOMAN COLLECTION.* Published Aug. 31, 1952, *THE DAILY OKLAHOMAN.*

Page 22 (right)

Construction of the Tulsa Cafe during the oil boom in Cromwell, 1925. *THE OKLAHOMAN COLLECTION.* Unpublished.

Page 23

The boomtown of Seminole is alive with (oil field) activity during the earlier part of this century. *THE OKLAHOMAN COLLECTION.* Published June 13, 1982. *THE DAILY OKLAHOMAN.*

Page 24

Oil field workers on the Britton-Olson Oil Company's Vanek No. One. Staff Photo by Alphia Hart, Aug. 7, 1938. *THE OKLAHOMAN COLLECTION.* Unpublished.

Page 25 (left)

The I.T.I.O. (Indian Territory Illuminating Oil and Foster Petroleum companies) well six miles south of Oklahoma City when it blew in as a gusher Tuesday afternoon. Staff Photo by Alvin Rucker. Published Dec. 5, 1928, *THE DAILY OKLAHOMAN.*

Page 25 (right)

The Oklahoma National Guard stands watch over the oil fields that surround the State Capitol, Oct. 31, 1939. *THE OKLAHOMAN COLLECTION.* Unpublished.

Page 26-27

A panoramic view of downtown Tulsa. *THE OKLAHOMAN COLLECTION.* Published Apr. 5, 1936, *THE DAILY OKLAHOMAN.*

Page 28 (left)

Stillwater's growth has been steady since the run (1889). *THE OKLAHOMAN COLLECTION.* Published Apr. 23, 1939, *THE DAILY OKLAHOMAN.*

Page 28 (right)

The Hotel Aldridge in downtown McAlester. Photo by the Brown Studio, June 4, 1931, *THE OKLAHOMAN COLLECTION.* Unpublished.

Page 29 (top)

The Belleview Mineral Plunge, Sulphur, Mar. 8, 1939. *THE OKLAHOMAN COLLECTION.* Unpublished.

Page 29 (left)

Plans are underway for a county-wide celebration of the Armistice day in El Reno when the new monument recently erected to the heroism of the men who went from Canadian county to do their part in the World war will be unveiled.

THE OKLAHOMAN COLLECTION. Published Nov. 3, 1931, *THE DAILY OKLAHOMAN.*

Page 30

Miners and rescue volunteers gather at the Old Town Mine disaster near McAlester. Nov. 29, 1930. *THE OKLAHOMAN COLLECTION.* Unpublished.

Page 31 (left)

Hours after 29 miners were entombed by a blast in the Wheatley No. 4 mine at McAlester Monday night, grim crews of rescue workers gathered at the mouth of the slope. Five rescue workers are shown in the foreground of this picture, waiting for a call to go below to replace comrades sickened by afterdamp. The man on the extreme right is looking down the slope bank for the cable cars from the depths. He is standing near the place where William Donely was when he was killed by the explosion. Staff Photo. Published Oct. 30, 1930, *THE DAILY OKLAHOMAN.*

Page 31 (top right)

Miners from the Old Town Coal Company mine disaster are buried in a mass grave in McAlester. Photo by the Brown Studio, Dec. 20, 1930, *THE OKLAHOMAN COLLECTION.* Unpublished.

Page 31 (bottom right)

Mrs. Irene Nigh and H.L. Martin, relief workers, are shown in the temporary kitchen set up to provide food for the rescue workers. Staff Photo. Published Oct. 29, 1930, *THE DAILY OKLAHOMAN.*

Page 32

A street scene in Rush Springs, the state's famous watermelon town; a day's production of some of the Rush Springs growers is shown in this picture. *THE OKLAHOMAN COLLECTION.* Published Sept. 6, 1936, *THE DAILY OKLAHOMAN.*

Page 33 (top)

Threshing scene, southwest of Guthrie in Logan county in this undated picture. Bryan Studio, Guthrie. *THE OKLAHOMAN COLLECTION.* Published Apr. 16, 1989. *THE SUNDAY OKLAHOMAN.*

Page 33 (bottom left)

Oklahoma farmers have reversed the old one about "making hay while the sun shines," having had enough of that Sunshine business during July and most of August, thank you. Now, they're plowing by moonlight, or, if there isn't any moonlight, by tractor light. The cameraman caught Albin Kastl breaking a field for the autumn wheat sowing on the Antone Dobry farm west of Yukon. Working against time, the tractor plows will break the 100 acres on the Dobry farm in four days. Staff Photo. Published Sept. 1, 1934, *THE DAILY OKLAHOMAN.*

Page 33 (bottom right)

This photo shows how the panhandle farmers are making deep furrows to receive and store moisture for feed crops. *THE OKLAHOMAN COLLECTION.* Published Mar. 18, 1934, *THE DAILY OKLAHOMAN.*

Page 34 (top left)

The Oklahoma State Indian Fair Association meeting at Craterville Park in this undated picture. *THE OKLAHOMAN COLLECTION.* Unpublished.

Page 34 (bottom left)

A group of Indians in front of a tipi at Craterville Park in this undated picture. *THE OKLAHOMAN COLLECTION.* Unpublished.

Page 34-35

The Board of Directors of the Oklahoma State Indian Fair Association in front of the loud speakers at the 4th annual fair held at Craterville Park. *THE OKLAHOMAN COLLECTION.* Published Aug. 8, 1931, *THE DAILY OKLAHOMAN.*

Page 36 (top)
Oklahoma City police chief John Watt bars all gadgets in cops shiny new scout cars as two unidentified police pose with the new cars in this photo taken Oct. 15, 1934, *THE OKLAHOMAN COLLECTION*. Unpublished.

Page 36 (center)
Hap Brisco (Oklahoma Highway Patrol) stands by headquarters trailer stationed in Lawton in 1937. *THE OKLAHOMAN COLLECTION*. Published July 7, 1960, *OKLAHOMA CITY TIMES*.

Page 36 (bottom)
Oklahoma City police scouts check over their equipment. *THE OKLAHOMAN COLLECTION*. Published Sept. 4, 1932, *THE DAILY OKLAHOMAN*.

Page 37
Left to right, O.F. Barnett, Ben Hart, O.R. Reed, Henry McMullen and L.D. Jenkins.; McMullen is the baby of the squad, tipping the scales at a mere 180 compared to Reed's 290. Average weight of the five, 229 pounds. *THE OKLAHOMAN COLLECTION*. Published Nov. 19, 1939, *THE DAILY OKLAHOMAN*.

Page 38 (top)
Wiley Post and Harold Gatty landing the *Winnie Mae* at Curtiss-Wright airport in Oklahoma City on July 10, 1931. *THE OKLAHOMAN COLLECTION*. Unpublished.

Page 38 (bottom)
A sleek blue monster will be dropping into Oklahoma City daily from now on, pulling the Frisco railway's Firefly streamliner on a seven-hour schedule between Oklahoma City and Kansas City. Staff Photo by C.J. Kaho. Published Mar. 29, 1940, *OKLAHOMA CITY TIMES*.

Page 39
Horse drawn buggies and their drivers watch as motorized automobiles parade on a brick lined street in downtown Guthrie in this undated picture. *THE OKLAHOMAN COLLECTION*. Unpublished.

Page 40 (left)
Will Rogers and Louise Dresser recreate a scene from the 1933 movie "State Fair" in this undated photo. *THE OKLAHOMAN COLLECTION*. Unpublished.

Page 40 (right)
The Criterion Theatre as it appeared as a showplace in the late 1920's. *THE OKLAHOMAN COLLECTION*. Published Feb. 2, 1973, *THE DAILY OKLAHOMAN*.

Page 41
Perhaps the 900 children who saw "Dead End" at the State theatre Saturday morning are now able to appreciate better the kind of life they can lead in this southwestern city. Included in the crowd which saw this popular movie free were the Kiwanis junior police, members of the South Side Kids club of the Y.M.C.A. and the Boy Scouts. T.B. Noble, jr., manager of theater acted as host. Staff Photo by Wm. J. Shroder, jr. Published Oct. 30, 1937, *THE DAILY OKLAHOMAN*.

Page 42
Edna Vance was better known to her WKY Radio kitchen audience as "Aunt Susan." She built the first radio kitchen in the nation and was also a cooking columnist for *The Daily Oklahoman* for 15 years. *THE OKLAHOMAN COLLECTION*. Unpublished.

Page 43 (top left)
Humorist and actor, Will Rogers, prepares his newspaper column using a typewriter while in the front seat of his auto in this undated photo. *THE OKLAHOMAN COLLECTION*. Unpublished.

Page 43 (top right)
News reel and still photographers line the federal courthouse in Oklahoma City during the Charles F. Urschel kidnapping trial. *THE OKLAHOMAN COLLECTION*. Published Oct. 8, 1933, *THE DAILY OKLAHOMAN*.

Page 43 (bottom left)
Copy editors prepare news stories for afternoon edition of the *Oklahoma City Times* in this 1938 photo. *THE OKLAHOMAN COLLECTION*. Unpublished.

Page 44
Bryant Baker, sculptor, in his New York studio, poses with the working model of the Pioneer Woman statue in this undated photo. *THE OKLAHOMAN COLLECTION*. Unpublished.

Page 45 (left)
Bryant Baker, sculptor, perched on top a 20-foot ladder cleaning the face of the bronze faces of the pioneer group. *THE OKLAHOMAN COLLECTION*. Published Mar. 27, 1930, *THE DAILY OKLAHOMAN*.

Page 45 (right)
Half of Oklahoma appeared to be clustered about the statue of the Pioneer Woman at Ponca City Tuesday afternoon when a *Daily Oklahoman* staff photographer, circling about in a plane snapped this picture of the throng. Staff Photo. Published Apr. 23, 1930, *THE DAILY OKLAHOMAN*.

Page 46 (top)
Families from across the state pay last respects to Oklahoma aviator Wiley Post lying in state at the Oklahoma State capitol. Aug. 22, 1935, *THE OKLAHOMAN COLLECTION*. Unpublished.

Page 46 (bottom)
Friends assist Mrs. Wiley Post, widow of the famous flyer, as she enters the First Baptist Church in Oklahoma City. Aug. 23, 1935. *THE OKLAHOMAN COLLECTION*. Unpublished.

Page 47
A highlight of Friday's ceremonies attending dedication of the Will Rogers memorial museum at Claremore was the unveiling of the imposing Rogers statue by Jo Davidson, famed sculptor. The comedian's daughter Mary, right, pulled the cord. Left to right are Davidson, Mrs. Oscar Lawler, Los Angeles, California, wife of Rogers' attorney; Lawler, directly behind her; Mrs. Sallie McSpadden, Chelsea, sister of Rogers; Jesse Jones, chairman of the Reconstruction Finance Corp, and chief speaker at the dedication; Pat Hurley, former secretary of war, Mrs. Betty Rogers and Governor (E.W.) Marland. Staff Photo. Published Nov. 4, 1938, *OKLAHOMA CITY TIMES*.

Page 48-49
THE WORLD AT YOUR FEET—The scenic road to the top of southwest Oklahoma's highest mountain, Mount Scott, northwest of Lawton in Comanche County, is completed. After three years of work, the drive will be opened for public use, without charge Sunday, George E. Mushbach, superintendent of the Wichita Mountains Wildlife Refuge, announced Thursday. The road climbs 1,000 feet above the valley below and in three miles winds to an elevation of 2,467 feet above sea level, spiraling around the mountain in three complete circuits. From the summit, where parking space for 200 cars is provided, a view of the surrounding mountains, lakes, and valleys of the game refuge can be obtained. Left, a car begins the climb up the new road. Center, a party pauses for a view of Lake Lawtonka. At the right, another view of the road and surrounding scenery. The entrance to the drive is three miles west of Medicine Park, 16 miles northwest of Lawton, and 12 miles northeast of Cache. *THE OKLAHOMAN COLLECTION*. Published Aug. 12, 1938, *THE DAILY OKLAHOMAN*.

they felt their area of town is ected until somebody wants thing.

Oklahoma City Mayor Ron Norick celebrates Tuesday night after voters approved the Metropolitan Area Projects plan. Nearly 54 percent of voters who cast ballots favored the $238 million proposition.

tossed out by a few dozen voters interviewed at various polling locations around the county during Tuesday's vote on a 1-cent sales tax

The second-term mayor was the key force behind work that led to Tuesday's proposition to finance new

by a five-year, 1-cent sales tax.

The plan passed 32,367 to 27,762 in unofficial returns

Page 50 (left)
Typical of many eroded Oklahoma acres is this land on the Eula Foreman farm about 20 miles west of Guthrie. Sloping to fill gullies and terraces would help reclamation. *THE OKLAHOMAN COLLECTION.* Published Apr. 7, 1940, *THE DAILY OKLAHOMAN.*

Page 50 (right)
Dust clouds rise over Hooker in Texas County on Apr. 14, 1935. *THE OKLAHOMAN COLLECTION.* Published Apr. 19, 1999, *THE SUNDAY OKLAHOMAN.*

Page 51
Howard Carleton in a strip of three-year-old trees east of Mangum. *THE OKLAHOMAN COLLECTION.* Published June 12, 1938, *THE DAILY OKLAHOMAN.*

Page 52-53
Northeastern Oklahoma's Grand River dam is becoming one of Oklahoma's top ranking tourist attractions, and no wonder. It is the most stupendous piece of construction ever undertaken in the state. The view above, from the downstream side, shows just how big the massive dam really is. The buttresses—there are 52 of them—will be 150 feet high, 24 feet wide, and have a base width of 206 feet. With the spillway and overflow sections of the dam included, the wall of concrete stretches continuously for 6,565 feet. Another set of arches will go on top of the buttresses to support a highway across the top of the dam, which will have a 24-foot roadway. The largest power and steam shovels in the southwest are being used in the construction, some of them 180 feet high. Contractors imported life nets used on the Golden Gate bridge to safeguard workmen who scramble around at dizzy heights but despite all precautions; eight workmen have been killed so far on the project. More electricity is required in the construction work than the entire amount used by the city of Vinita. *THE OKLAHOMAN COLLECTION.* Published Sept. 16, 1938, *OKLAHOMA CITY TIMES.*

Page 54 (left)
ALL PLAQUED UP—If there is any doubt in the future about who did the work on more than 300 new school buildings, bridges, community houses, city halls and armories in Oklahoma, it won't be the fault of the works progress administration. Bronze plaques similar to the one displayed by Miss Helen Ellegood, WPA secretary, are being placed on all the WPA-built structures this week. Staff photo by C.J. Kaho. Published June 10, 1936, *THE DAILY OKLAHOMAN.*

Pages 54 and 55 (top)
Oklahoma City Orchestra and city wide massed chorus performs for National Music Week concert in the Municipal Auditorium, May 8, 1940. *THE OKLAHOMAN COLLECTION.* Unpublished.

Page 54 (bottom left)
FOR UNCLE SAM—No wonder professional showmen are beginning to worry about the encroachment of Uncle Sam on their premises. Spending an average of $2,739 a month for salaries of one Oklahoma troupe, including a bevy of beautiful girls like those above, the government is apt to give George White, Billy Rose and the rest of the boys some worries, and may even effect a revival of the bald-headed row in the hinterlands. These girls comprise the chorus for "Hollywood Cabaret," to be presented by the Works Progress Administration at the Shrine auditorium Friday and Saturday nights and Sunday afternoon. They were caught during rehearsal Monday by the photographer, but by opening night they'll have government-purchased costumes, costing $180, flimsy and abbreviated enough to do justice to a promoter less dignified than Uncle Sam. Staff Photo by C.J. Kaho. Published Sept. 1, 1936, *THE DAILY OKLAHOMAN.*

Page 54 (bottom right)
President Franklin D. Roosevelt, on the arm of his son James, waves to the crowd at the Oklahoma Fair grounds July 9, 1938. *THE OKLAHOMAN COLLECTION.* Unpublished.

Page 56-57
A modernistic panoramic view looking toward the east of downtown Oklahoma City. *THE OKLAHOMAN COLLECTION.* Published Sept. 27, 1936, *THE DAILY OKLAHOMAN.*

CHAPTER THREE
A NEW FRONTIER

Page 58
New battalion mass formation of infantry troops was employed by the 45th Infantry Division for the first time in formal review at Camp Barkeley, Texas, Friday. The formation consists of a "box" of 1,000 men marching 48 abreast to form one large unit. 45th Infantry Division Photo/*THE OKLAHOMAN COLLECTION.* Published May 31, 1941, *OKLAHOMA CITY TIMES.*

Page 59
"You know, Charlie," mused the governor Monday night as he surveyed the seam-busting crowd at the auditorium, " I never knew of but one other little man who could draw a mob like this." Charlie naturally, was curious. "The other little man," grinned the governor, "was Mr. Dewey." Cynical Republicans wondered how the governor knew, because he wasn't even in town when Dewey packed the auditorium for a campaign speech last summer. Anyhow, that sort of badinage went on as Governor Kerr, Charlie McCarthy and Edgar Bergen mugged shamelessly for the cameraman. Staff Photo by Bill Stockwell. Published May 22, 1945, *THE DAILY OKLAHOMAN.*

Page 60
The 45th Infantry Division early morning revelry at Ft. Sill, Oklahoma, in this undated photo. 45th Infantry Division Photo/*THE OKLAHOMAN COLLECTION.* Unpublished.

Page 61
The 45th Infantry Division parades down Broadway in downtown Oklahoma City in this June 22, 1940, picture. *THE OKLAHOMAN COLLECTION.* Unpublished.

Page 62
The 45th Infantry Division set up camp on their way to Louisiana for maneuvers. 45th Infantry Division Photo/*THE OKLAHOMAN COLLECTION.* Published Aug. 9, 1941, *OKLAHOMA CITY TIMES.*

Page 63 (left and center)
Members of the 45th Infantry Division trained in all types of weather as shown by these two unidentified soldiers while on maneuvers. 45th Infantry Division Photo/*THE OKLAHOMAN COLLECTION.* Unpublished.

Page 63 (right)
Bill Mauldin, a member of the 45th Infantry Division, became famous with his "Willy and Joe" cartoons, later winning Mauldin the Pulitzer Prize. *THE OKLAHOMAN COLLECTION.* Unpublished.

Page 64 (left)
Time was when Mrs. Lo Dema Davis of Colony thought helping her husband run their 925-acre farm was a full-time job. But then she discovered the monkey wrench and what it could do to a landing gear. Now she lives in Oklahoma City, and has been working at the (Tinker) field a week. Hubby is running the farm these days. *THE OKLAHOMAN COLLECTION.* Published June 4, 1942, *THE DAILY OKLAHOMAN.*

Page 64 (right)
B-24 aircraft undergo modification at Tinker Field in 1943. *THE OKLAHOMAN COLLECTION.* Unpublished.

Page 65
Busy crews on the assembly line of the Douglas Aircraft Company Oklahoma City plant bend to their work making installations of C-47 cockpit enclosures. Center wings of the big "Skytrain" military cargo version of the DC-3 airliner, hulk above them in the background of the "moving" line of this large midwestern plant which completed an outstanding first-year production record this month. Douglas Aircraft Company Oklahoma City Plant/*THE OKLAHOMAN COLLECTION.* Published Apr. 16, 1989, *THE SUNDAY OKLAHOMAN.*

Page 66

Having heard that scrap was needed, the little McClain county city of Blanchard decided Wednesday was as good a day as any to get it in. So for five hours in the afternoon the town shut up tight and everybody pitched in. At the end of the day, this was the result – a pile half a block long on Main Street. Best estimates were that the scrap pile would total 65 or 70 tons—not bad. Staff Photo. Published Oct. 1, 1942, *THE DAILY OKLAHOMAN*.

Page 67 (top)

This vast store of scrap rubber tires, contained in a 17 acre "bin" in Packingtown, is being held on call by various processing plants which are reclaiming rubber to make "new" Victory tires for motorists. Much of this scrap pile may never be used, however, if the synthetic plants get into production as planned by October. Staff Photo by Bill Stockwell. Published Jan. 27, 1943, *THE DAILY OKLAHOMAN*.

Page 67 (bottom)

This little heap contains 80 tons of scrap to throw at the axis, and is on its way to them now. The scrap was accumulated in the Guy R. Lanman iron foundry in El Reno over a period of three years. Monday, it was loaded into two railroad cars and shipped off to the steel mills. This pile contains only steel; another of equal size was all cast iron. Staff Photo by Betty Baughman. Published Oct. 6, 1942, *THE DAILY OKLAHOMAN*.

Page 68

Life of an aviation cadet isn't all the study of aviation and flying roaring planes. This class at Enid Army Flying School is being initiated into the mysteries of radio code transmission and reception. Soon their "skull" work will be practiced in the air. *THE OKLAHOMAN COLLECTION*. Published May 16, 1942, *THE DAILY OKLAHOMAN*.

Page 69 (left)

Acting Sergeant Gladys Lancaster, guest of Cadet David E. Griffiths, is being shown around the post by her host and some of her admirers. Miss Lancaster is the first WAAC visitor at the Enid Army Flying School. She is on furlough from Fort Des Moines, Iowa, where she is stationed as a drill sergeant. Cadet Griffiths is a member of the 43-D class at this basic flying training school. *THE OKLAHOMAN COLLECTION*. Unpublished.

Page 69 (right)

Here for a three-day short course before being assigned to recruiting sub-stations in the state, the seven WAAC officers shown above Thursday were learning how to make their civilian sisters see the light. They will be sent to sub-stations near their home towns on the theory they will be most effective working with women they know. From front to back they are Carla McGee, Blackwell; Massye Goins, Fairland; Erme Hite, Oklahoma City; Jean Newell, Tulsa; Viola Kinnard, Randlett; Lillian Corley, Oklahoma City; and Ida Madden, Hollis. All are third officers or lieutenants. Staff Photo by C.J. Kaho. Published June 11, 1943, *OKLAHOMA CITY TIMES*.

Page 70 (top)

Army Air Corp pilots undergo flight training at Muskogee Army Flying School in this undated picture. *THE OKLAHOMAN COLLECTION*. Unpublished.

Page 70 (bottom)

Lieut. Valentine Brown, assistant squadron operations officer at Will Rogers field, has seen to it that some of his men are going to be ready when an alert sounds. To teach his service group combat duty, Lieutenant Brown uses a dummy .30-caliber machine gun mounted on a large "tug"—used ordinarily for heavy pulling jobs at the base. Staff Photo. Published Sept. 5, 1942, *OKLAHOMA CITY TIMES*.

Page 71 (left)

Sgt. Max Kaminski, after packing his own parachute, made his first jump at Will Rogers field. Staff Photo. Published Nov. 5, 1941, *THE DAILY OKLAHOMAN*.

Page 71 (right)

Here's where a soldier must really strong-arm his way across. Jumping to reach the bars, he must swing from bar to bar, Tarzan fashion, without touching the ground beneath him. Staff Photo. Published June 12, 1942, *OKLAHOMA CITY TIMES*.

CONGRESSIONAL MEDAL
OF HONOR WINNERS

Page 72 (bottom right)

A hero to all Lexington children, (Major) John Smith's particularly one to his nieces, Virginia, 9 years old, and Marian, 8 years old, daughters of Mr. and Mrs. Robert O. Smith, Jr. Their daddy is county attorney for Cleveland County. Staff Photo by Bill Stockwell. Published Jan. 3, 1942, *THE DAILY OKLAHOMAN*.

Page 73 (left)

Broken Arrow turned out Wednesday to give a hero's welcome to Lieut. Ernest Childers, 45th Infantry Division hero. Shown riding the parade with Ernest is his brother Clarence of Tulsa. Staff Photo by Joe Miller. Published Apr. 27, 1944. *THE DAILY OKLAHOMAN*.

Page 73 (top right)

Robert Rivers holds a picture of his brother, Ruben, which was taken shortly before the young solider died in 1944. Staff Photo. Published Jan. 14, 1967, *THE DAILY OKLAHOMAN*.

The following information was taken and condensed from official military records.

Page 72-73

2nd Lt. Ernest Childers, 45th Infantry Division, received the CMH for conspicuous gallantry at Oliveto, Italy, Sept. 22, 1943. He was born at Broken Arrow. Published Apr. 27, 1944, *THE DAILY OKLAHOMAN*.

S/Sgt. John R. Crews, Co. F, 253d Infantry, 63d Infantry Division, was the recipient of the CMH for his heroism near Lebenbacherhof, Germany, Apr. 8, 1945. He was born at Golden. Published June 23, 1948, *THE DAILY OKLAHOMAN*.

Commander Ernest E. Evans, commanding officer of the *U.S.S. Johnston*, received the CMH for conspicuous gallantry against the Japanese fleet during the battle off Samar, Oct. 25, 1944. He was born at Pawnee. Published Dec. 9, 1945, *THE DAILY OKLAHOMAN*.

1st Lt. Donald J. Gott, 452d Bombardment Group, 8th Air Force, was awarded the CMH for heroism displayed after his B-17 was severely damaged during a bomb run on Saarbrucken, Germany, Nov. 9, 1944. He was born at Arnett. Published June 18, 1945, *THE DAILY OKLAHOMAN*.

Pvt. Harold G. Kiner, Co. F, 117th Infantry, 30th Infantry Division, was awarded the CMH for sacrificing his life by falling on a hand grenade to save two comrades near Palenburg, Germany, Oct. 2, 1944. He was born at Aline. (No photograph available). Story published June 3, 1945, *THE DAILY OKLAHOMAN*.

Lt. Richard Miles McCool, Jr., USN, commanding officer of the *U.S.S. LSC-122*, received the CMH for his courageous action during operations against Japanese forces off Okinawa, June 10-11, 1945. He was born in Tishomingo but entered the service in Ohio. (No photograph available). Story published Dec. 19, 1945, *THE DAILY OKLAHOMAN*.

Sgt. Troy A. McGill, Troop G, 5th Cavalry Regiment, 1st Cavalry Division, was awarded the CMH for his heroism in action against enemy forces on Los Negros Islands, Admiralty Group, Mar. 4, 1944. He was born in Knoxville, TN, but entered the Army at Ada. (No photograph available). Story published June 1, 1944, *THE DAILY OKLAHOMAN*.

1st Lt. Jack C. Montgomery, 45th Infantry Division, received the CMH for gallantry in action near Padiglione, Italy, Feb. 22, 1944. He was born at Long. Published July 14, 1946, *THE DAILY OKLAHOMAN.*

Pfc. Manuel Perez, Jr., Co. A, 511th Parachute Infantry, was awarded the CMH for courageous determination and heroic disregard of grave danger Feb. 13, 1945, making it possible to advance his unit toward a valuable objective on Luson, Philippine Islands. He was born in Oklahoma City and entered the service in Chicago, IL. Published July 20, 1945, *THE DAILY OKLAHOMAN.*

Pfc. John N. Reese, Jr., Co. B, 148th Infantry, 37th Infantry Division, received the CMH for his bravery in the attack on 300 enemy troops at Paco Railroad Station, Manila, P.I., Feb. 9, 1945. He was born in Muskogee. (No photograph available). Story published Apr. 5, 1959, *THE DAILY OKLAHOMAN.*

S.Sgt. Ruben Rivers, Co. A, 761st Tank Battalion, 3rd Army, was awarded the CMH for conspicuous gallantry and intrepidity in action at the risk of life and above and beyond the call of duty Nov. 19, 1944, during action in France. His family received the medal 53 years later. Rivers was one of the first of seven Black soldiers awarded the Medal of Honor. No Black Americans were awarded the medal during World War II despite numerous acts of heroism. Published June 14, 1997, *THE DAILY OKLAHOMAN.*

Pfc. Henry Schauer, 3d Infantry Division, U.S. Army, was awarded the CMH for conspicuous gallantry and intrepidity at risk of life and above and beyond the call of duty May 23, 1944, near Cisterna di Littoria, Italy. He was born in Clinton but entered the service at Scobey, Mont. (No photograph available). Story published June 10, 1945, *THE DAILY OKLAHOMAN.*

Pfc. Albert Earnest Schwab, USMCR, received the CMH for conspicuous gallantry and loss of life in action against Japanese forces on Okinawa Shima in the Ryukyu Islands, May 7, 1945. He was born in Washington, D.C., but joined the Marines in Tulsa. (No photograph available). Story published June 2, 1946, *THE DAILY OKLAHOMAN.*

Major John L. Smith, USMC, Marine Fighting Squadron 223, was awarded the CMH for his heroic achievements in aerial combat and shooting down 16 Japanese planes in the Solomon Islands area, Aug. 21 and Sept. 15, 1942. He was born at Lexington. Published Jan. 17, 1943, *THE DAILY OKLAHOMAN.*

Capt. Jack L. Treadwell, Co. F, 180th Infantry, 45th Infantry Division, received the CMH for single-handedly capturing six pillboxes and 18 prisoners near Nieder-Wurzbach, Germany, Mar. 18, 1945. He was born in Alabama but entered the Army from Snyder. Published Nov. 15, 1945, *THE DAILY OKLAHOMAN.*

Lt. Col. Leon R. Vance, Jr., 489th Bomber Group, U.S. Army Corps, received the CMH for leading an attack June 5, 1944, against defended enemy coastal positions in the vicinity of Wimereaux, France. He then returned the crew to a point where they could bail out with safety before the crippled aircraft was ditched. He was born at Enid but entered the service in New York. Published Jan. 15, 1945, *THE DAILY OKLAHOMAN.*

Page 74
The war was ending in Europe in the spring of 1945, as members of the 45th Infantry Division paused to give thanks in the ruins of a German community. *THE OKLAHOMAN COLLECTION.* Unpublished.

Page 75
Traffic simply stopped at the corner of Main and Robinson in downtown Oklahoma City on Aug. 14, 1945, when victory over Japan was declared. The flash announcing it was all over came about 4 p.m. Within minutes, shouting throngs were dancing in the streets, hurling confetti and stopping traffic. Staff Photo by Bill Stockwell. Published Aug. 19, 1945, *THE DAILY OKLAHOMAN.*

Page 76
Postmaster, Ardil Meeks hands a letter to one of his nearly 400 post office customers in the rural community of Hennepin. Staff Photo by Bill Johnson. Published Sept. 25, 1949, *THE DAILY OKLAHOMAN.*

Page 77 (left)
Waning summer is bringing a change only of degree in the lives of some Oklahomans who, having the means, enjoy some of the state's outdoor beauty to the fullest. One place they do it is Grand Lake. More of a playground for Tulsa and northeast Oklahoma than for Oklahoma City, Grand Lake is a truly beautiful spot in the state's scenic mosaic. Tulsa folk make the most of it. Many wealthy Tulsans maintain permanent homes there, some of which are elaborate and expensive. Pictured here is the private dock below the home of Robert M. Siegfried, an insurance executive. Hopkins Photography/*THE OKLAHOMAN COLLECTION.* Published Sept. 17, 1950, *THE DAILY OKLAHOMAN.*

Page 77 (right)
Del City, two miles east of Eastern on SE 29, which two years ago was a vast wheat field. Developed by George Epperly, the huge tract now contains 400 completed homes and 200 more are going up. Staff Photo. Published July 11, 1948, *THE DAILY OKLAHOMAN.*

Page 78 (left)
Prentice Gautt, became the first black football player at the University of Oklahoma. Staff Photo. Published Sept. 3, 1958, *THE DAILY OKLAHOMAN.*

Page 78 (right)
JUBILATION REIGNS ON THE OU BENCH as the Sooners score their final touchdown Saturday in a 56-21 rout of Colorado. Coach Bud Wilkinson leads the cheering while line coach Gomer Jones appears weeping from joy. Identifiable players are Bob Timberlake, (81), Tulsa end; Gerald McPhail, (48), Oklahoma City back; and Delbert Long, (27), Ponca City end. Staff Photo by Joe Miller. Published Oct. 23, 1955, *THE DAILY OKLAHOMAN.*

Page 79
"So that's the way they have us ranked?" the Oklahoma A&M basketball team seems to be saying as it looks over coach Hank Iba's shoulders at a national magazine early-season cage survey. In the back row from the left are Gerald Stockton, John Miller, Ken Hicks, Bob Seymour and Kendall Sheets. Seated in the row back of Iba are Keith Smith, Bob Pager, Pete Darcey, Gale McArthur, Norm Pilgrim and Emmett McAfee. The Aggies play a return match with Arkansas Thursday night in Fayetteville and Saturday night take on Southern Methodist in Stillwater. Staff Photo. Published Dec. 13, 1950, *THE DAILY OKLAHOMAN.*

Page 80
Frightened cow is now perfectly content in her circular cell. Staff Photo by Joe Miller. Published Feb. 25, 1949, *THE DAILY OKLAHOMAN.*

Page 81 (top left)
Yukon farmer, Bill Mach, tries to coach his stuck cow, Grady, through a small opening in the grain elevator. Staff Photo by George Tapscott, Feb. 27, 1949, *THE OKLAHOMAN COLLECTION.* Unpublished.

Page 81 (top right)
Dr. L.J. Crump uses a hypo to relax her. Staff Photo. Published Feb. 27, 1949, *THE DAILY OKLAHOMAN.*

Page 81 (bottom left)
Everybody always tries to get in the act. After Grady was released from solitary Saturday, she went outside for a breath of fresh air. Bill Mach, her owner, is on the left. The others are well wishers who came to see her com-

ing-out party, which was a slippery success. Staff Photo by George Tapscott. Feb. 26, 1949, *OKLAHOMA CITY TIMES*.

Page 82

A HEAP OF WORK, much of it behind the scenes, is needed to get an airline passenger airborne. Above is the reception committee you'd find at boarding time if you met everyone who made a flight possible. Employment in the thousands is possible because of aviation here. Pictured here are Mark Burke, Bob Smith, Susie Wilcox, John Hamilton, Morris Hanes, James Marsh, R.L. Frederick, Lavonne E. Hatfield, Wayne R. Laub, C.E. Coffelt, Doug Hanna, A.J. Allen, Henry Martin, L.H. Pendergraft, Alajandro Elespuru, Alvin Pecena, Paul Kinney, Leon May, J.L. Horton, Jack Garner, Frank Burns, Jim W. Moore, Charles N. Sarsycki, Helen Reed, Marrion Whaley, Guinevere Gardner, Geneva Wood, George Hukill, Lucy Elliott, Clara Holloway, William Staltari, William O. Coleman, Lou Dahl, Ernest J. Verba, M.O. Huntress, C. G. Heckes, A.C. Starwalt, Flo Self, Gilbert Smart, Lloyd P. Richey, George Starwalt, V.W. Brown, Joe Flynn, Dennis Burk, Mattie Kerney, Cliston McGlory, R.A. Hodder, Sharon Meaders, Larry Bushnell, Dean Daugherty, Fred Kennedy, Tom Hanges, Vernol Melton, Al Smith, Nancy Senit, Virginia Walker, Howard Taylor, Leonard B. Haggard, Arch B. Moody, Virgil G. Hawk and Clara Mae Capps. Staff Photo by Dick Peterson. Published Dec. 14, 1957, *OKLAHOMA CITY TIMES*.

Page 83

Tomorrow's train today, is the Rock Island's Jet Rocket on display in the railroad show of the (Semi-Centennial) exposition. The lightweight train weighs half as much as a standard, and cost about half as much and operates more economically. Staff Photo. Published June 16, 1957, *THE DAILY OKLAHOMAN*.

Page 83 (top right)

Interurban cars, buses and trolleys mingled in this Oklahoma Railway Terminal on Grand Avenue (now Sheridan) in 1940. It was a busy place as workers transferred from one route to another going to and from work. Preston George photo/*THE OKLAHOMAN COLLECTION*. Published Mar. 25, 1980, *THE DAILY OKLAHOMAN*.

Page 84

This junior high band group at Douglass high school has no classroom. W.E. Perry, teacher, holds sessions for 120 pupils per day in a basement corridor between the gymnasium and dressing rooms. Oklahoma county residents will have a chance to remedy these overcrowded conditions Dec. 11 when they vote on the $7 million bond issue, including $900,000 for a new Negro senior high school. Staff Photo by Richard Peterson. Published Dec. 2, 1951, *THE DAILY OKLAHOMAN*.

Page 85 (left)

Mechanical things interest these Navajos and they have learned about tractor maintenance and servicing at Chilocco. Here Neil Roanhorse, Chambers, Ariz., and Joe Capitan, Gallup, N.M., gas up a tractor. Staff Photo by Bill Johnson. Published May 21, 1950, *THE DAILY OKLAHOMAN*.

Page 85 (right)

Mrs. Marvin Hogue's portable schoolroom at Creston Hills is one of five at that overcrowded east side school, and of 27 which dot school sites over the city. They will be obsolete as soon as the school building program starts next autumn. These portable units are bright-walled rooms with plenty of windows. Floors are somewhat rougher than in the regular classroom, but book cases and blackboards are among the equipment. Some are steam heated, others have "pot bellied" stoves for radiation. Teachers agree that they are satisfactory emergency class housing, but are inconvenient because children must go to the main school building to fountains and toilets. Staff Photo by Bill Stockwell. Published Feb. 8, 1946, *OKLAHOMA CITY TIMES*.

Page 86 (top left)

Survivors of the Woodward tornado, including an elderly man who suffered a cut on his head during the storm, enjoy a meal brought in and prepared by volunteers at a shelter. The Woodward County town of 5,500 was devastated by the Apr. 9, 1947, tornado, which was on the ground for more than six hours, traveling more than 200 miles from the Texas Panhandle into Kansas. Staff Photo by Richard Meeks. Published Apr. 24, 1994, special section, *THE DAILY OKLAHOMAN*.

Page 86 (bottom left)

Mrs. Henry Skinner, one of the dozens of Woodward tornado victims who want to rebuild as soon as the remains of their houses are cleared away, searches through the wreckage of her two-story home for usable articles. She examines the battered kiddie-car of one of her children. Staff Photo by Al McLaughlin. Published Apr. 26, 1947, *THE DAILY OKLAHOMAN*.

Page 86 (right)

The west and north sections of Woodward bore the brunt of Wednesday night's storm. Aerial picture looks west from the business district. Staff Photo. Published Apr. 11, 1947, *THE DAILY OKLAHOMAN*.

Page 87 (top)

The Woodward County courthouse and the once-beautiful trees surrounding it were left devastated. The roof and all the windows were gone, and part of the cornice was pushed off the wall. Staff Photo. Published Apr. 10, 1947, *OKLAHOMA CITY TIMES*.

Page 87 (bottom left)

Don Roberson and his wife are without a home, but feel lucky to be alive. They were waiting for some friends from El Reno to come and get them to provide temporary shelter when this was taken. He is an employee of Carter Oil Co. Staff Photo by Richard B. Meeks. Published Apr. 11, 1947, *THE DAILY OKLAHOMAN*.

Page 88 (left)

Monday, the division held a final review. Kin and generals looked on as officers marched by. Equipment already had been shipped. Along the parade route, wives and sweethearts took pictures. Staff Photo. Published May 1, 1951, *THE DAILY OKLAHOMAN*.

Page 88 (center)

Little Larry Shough, 20 months, gazes pensively into space while his mother and dad cling to each other. They are Sgt.1/c and Mrs. Billy W. Shough, Elk City. Mrs. Shough and Billy arrived at Fort Sill early. Staff Photo. Published May 11, 1952, *THE DAILY OKLAHOMAN*.

Page 88 (right)

RETURNING THUNDERBIRD MEETS SON FOR FIRST TIME M-Sgt. Ray Mathis, Hollis, gets his first look at 6 months old Charles Ray, born while he was overseas with the 45th Infantry Division. It was an exciting moment for the sergeant and his wife, Doris. Staff Photo. Published Apr. 17, 1952, *OKLAHOMA CITY TIMES*.

Page 89 (left)

Wives and children threw themselves into the arms of the Thunderbird veterans who arrived at Will Rogers field Monday. Above, Mrs. and Martha Lynn race to meet W/Off. Francis A. Wolfe, who met them half way. Staff Photo by Bill Burns. Published Apr. 15, 1952, *THE DAILY OKLAHOMAN*.

Page 89 (center)

'Daddy' Is Her Birthday Present: Thursday was an unusually exciting day in the life of blonde Minnie Leona Woods of Lawton. Early this morning her mother took her to the railroad station at Fort Sill to greet a near stranger called "Daddy" in the person of Sgt. Homer Woods. Later in the day, Minnie was due to blow out two candles on her birthday cake. Sgt. Woods timed his arrival perfectly—with the unknowing aid of the army—landing at Sill with other homecoming 45th Infantry

Division Thunderbirds on his daughter's second birthday. His wife, Violet, is shown helping the sergeant get a hug from his youngster. Staff Photo. Published Apr. 17, 1952, *OKLAHOMA CITY TIMES*.

Page 89 (right)
Carl Ray, 3, wore the bright satin jacket his dad, Sgt. 1-C Eldon Montgomery, sent him from Japan, when he met the train Thursday morning at Fort Sill. Montgomery (who jumped off the train at Sill, had to get back on) was the first Thunderbird off the train Thursday morning— even before the wheels stopped turning. Staff Photo. Published Apr. 12, 1952, *OKLAHOMA CITY TIMES*.

Page 90
For the second straight day Oklahoma City stockyards were visited by more than 1,000 truckloads of cattle, biggest daily receipts since December. This picture shows part of the trucks which unloaded here Tuesday. Start of the season for delivery of cattle fattened and ready for slaughter plus late delivery of cattle, which need a little more fattening, was given for the reason. Cattle pasturage was poor because of winter and early spring drought. Some late deliveries were also believed caused by unsettled arguments over proposed beef price rollbacks. Staff Photo by Richard Peterson. Published July 11, 1951, *THE DAILY OKLAHOMAN*.

Page 91 (left)
Cattle pens at the Oklahoma City stockyards were filling up on Monday as cattle and calf receipts threatened to be the highest in stockyards history. Clarence Achgill, managing editor of the Oklahoma Livestock News, estimated cattle receipts at 10,500 head and the number of calves at 1,500. This would be slightly less than the 11,969 cattle and 3,092 calves sold on Aug. 26, 1946. However Achgill said country sales and packing house purchases could run the grand total to a record 17,000 head. Staff Photo by Richard Peterson. Published Sept. 9, 1952, *THE DAILY OKLAHOMAN*.

Page 91 (right)
Trucks loaded with cattle form a two block long line into the Oklahoma National Stock Yards in Oklahoma City. Staff Photo by Thomas F. Killian. *THE OKLAHOMAN COLLECTION*. Unpublished.

Page 92 (top)
Automotive hearts should leap with joy at this scene, showing laying of the first paving on the Oklahoma City end of the Turner turnpike Friday morning. Here Metropolitan Paving Co. workmen spread a five-inch layer of asphaltic concrete beginning at Mile No. 7, some 15 miles northeast of Oklahoma City. They will spread the ribbon back toward the city to Witcher, where the Oklahoma City toll gate will be built, and where the super-highway connects with an already built four-lane leading to the east end of Oklahoma City's U.S. 66 bypass. Staff Photo by Joe Miller. Published Aug. 16, 1952, *OKLAHOMA CITY TIMES*.

Page 92 (bottom left)
There aren't many who'd want to risk their personal cars to duplicate the fete, but toll road officials and newsmen have toured the Oklahoma City-Tulsa super-highway now under construction to get a picture of what it's like at this stage. A station wagon they used is shown on a particularly rough stretch of road just west of Bristow. Staff Photo by Bob Albright. Published May 30, 1952, *OKLAHOMA CITY TIMES*.

Page 92 (bottom right)
The Turner Turnpike turnstiles have been clicking with ever-increasing regularity since the opening year. Here Bunny Sanders checks through the toll road gate, receiving a ticket from Ted Swingle. Staff Photo. Published Mar. 8, 1959, *THE DAILY OKLAHOMAN*.

Page 93
Motorists ribbon-cutting ceremonies at the west gate of the turner turnpike, May 16, 1953. Inside the gate, a caravan of official cars headed for ceremonies at Stroud. Staff Photo by Bob Hauton. *THE OKLAHOMAN COLLECTION*. Unpublished.

Page 94
Mrs. Ben Austin Jr. dons a helmet to show fourth-grade students at Soldier Creek school equipment necessary in case of air raid or tornado. Staff Photo. Published Jan. 12, 1955, *OKLAHOMA CITY TIMES*.

Page 95 (left)
Mrs. Kermit Ingham, wife of a Stillwater lumberman, is safely lowered from the third story of a burning building (In this Civil Defense simulated training photo). Guiding the lashed victim to safety are Russell Martin, left, Stillwater school teacher, and Sham Sooter, civil air patrol leader. Staff Photo. Published Jan. 18, 1959, *THE DAILY OKLAHOMAN*.

Page 95 (top right)
Men get in the act too, Kenneth Wagner, Carl Kickingbird and Harry Tammen man stretcher on truck. Staff Photo by Cliff King. Published Feb. 5, 1959, *OKLAHOMA CITY TIMES*.

Page 95 (bottom right)
Not too many mayors in Oklahoma have taken time out to participate in civil defense training, but Stillwater Mayor A. B. Alcott, right, is in the Stillwater CD organization. Alcott and Mrs. C. D. Thomas try their hand at operating geiger counters. Staff Photo. Published Jan. 18, 1959, *THE DAILY OKLAHOMAN*.

Page 96 (left)
NEW LOOK IN POLIO VACCINATIONS in city schools are the little tykes who have to be held in mothers' arms while they get a shot of vaccine. This is graphic evidence they misunderstand the life-saving motives of Mrs. L. E. Base, city health nurse. Mrs. Helen Flud holds Alan, 20 months. A bottle of milk soothed his ruffled feelings a minute later. Staff Photo by Bob Albright. Published May 10, 1956, *OKLAHOMA CITY TIMES*.

Page 96 (center)
It's hard for a 10-year-old girl to understand that it takes a needle to help immunize her against polio. Angela Roberts, daughter of Mr. and Mrs. L. R. Roberts, Bethany, just hid her face and hoped for the best. Staff Photo by Bob Albright. Published Apr. 18. 1955, *OKLAHOMA CITY TIMES*.

Page 96 (right)
Calm and unflinching, 7-year old Connie Koettel takes her initial shot against paralytic polio and makes history by becoming one of the first Oklahoma youngsters to receive the successful Salk Vaccine. She is a pupil at Midwest City's Glendale elementary, one of six centers where vaccine was given Monday to 2,758 children. Staff Photo by George Tapscott. Published Apr. 19, 1955, *THE DAILY OKLAHOMAN*.

Page 97
Staging a rush on Oklahoma county's supply of Salk polio vaccine Monday evening, 7,000 persons showed up at Northeast high school. Staff Photo. Published July 28, 1959, *THE DAILY OKLAHOMAN*.

Page 98 (left)
Women as well as men are included among the 350 employees working on various assemblies of the new Aero Commander at the Tulakes factory. Above, Lena Pollack, left, and Laretha Whitson, are on the job. Staff Photo. Published Oct. 28, 1951, *THE DAILY OKLAHOMAN*.

Page 98 (top right)
Aircraft workers assemble planes at Aero Design & Engineering in this July 3, 1958, picture. Staff Photo. *THE OKLAHOMAN COLLECTION*. Unpublished.

Page 98 (bottom right)
Compact is the word for this assembly line. Planes are just as close together as they look to be in this picture. Staff Photo by Dick Peterson. Published Aug. 17, 1954, *OKLAHOMA CITY TIMES*.

Page 99 (left)
An example of the "crossbar" electro-mechanical switching equipment to be manufactured at the $35 million Western Electric plant here. Pictured is some of the crossbar equipment, which is used at the Southwestern Bell Telephone Co. in Oklahoma City. Switchman Jim Bessley carries out an inspection. Staff Photo. Published Mar. 7, 1957, *THE DAILY OKLAHOMAN*.

Page 99 (right)
Touring the huge Western Electric Co. plant here Tuesday, chamber of commerce members watch a woman operator turn out electric coils on a machine. Staff Photo. Published May 25 1960, *THE DAILY OKLAHOMAN*.

Page 100 (left)
Trainer, Bert Pettus, introduces Judy the elephant to Oklahoma City Zoo visitors Mar. 21, 1951. Staff Photo. *THE OKLAHOMAN COLLECTION*. Unpublished.

Page 100 (right)
Most of the youngsters at Judy the elephant's commencement Tuesday wanted the graduate to take them for a ride. But their reactions, when placed atop Judy's shoulders, were varied. Here, Judy's trainer, Bert Pettus, steadies 4-year-old Tommy Cain, who decided that Judy swayed too much. "Hold still Judy," he cried. He is the son of Mr. and Mrs. M.R. Cain of Perry—where the ceremony took place. Staff Photo. Published Mar. 21, 1951, *THE DAILY OKLAHOMAN*.

Page 101
A major attraction at the Oklahoma City zoo was monkey island in this Oct. 12, 1951, picture. Staff Photo by A.Y. Owen. *THE OKLAHOMAN COLLECTION*. Unpublished.

Page 102 (top)
Bumper cars at Wedgewood Village draw young and old alike. Staff Photo. Published Apr. 4, 1959, *THE DAILY OKLAHOMAN*.

Page 102 (bottom left)
It may get cold enough to freeze the steam from your coffee cup this winter, but there'll be a drive-in movie open within easy reach of your home. Staff Photo by Dick Peterson. Published Nov. 10, 1955, *OKLAHOMA CITY TIMES*.

Page 102 (bottom right)
THE FLYING SCOOTER, one of Wedgewood Village's two newest rides, is just as exciting as the riders want to make it. By grasping the forward fin a rider can provide his own self-propelled thrills as the "scooter" swings around the huge circle. Another ride is the new 1,800 Turnpike complete with safety-bumper sleek miniature autos. Staff Photo. Published June 21, 1959, *THE DAILY OKLAHOMAN*.

Page 103
Oklahoma City's Symphony Funday drew a throng of vacationing youngsters to Spinglake Park Wednesday. Published June 9, 1960, *THE DAILY OKLAHOMAN*.

Page 104
Oriental influence is seen in this kitchen decor, which is one of a group of seven being shown in the Parade of Industry building at the Oklahoman Semi-Centennial exposition. The cabinets are in a spring violet with the wall done in a sky blue color. It features a beam ceiling with the lighting woven into it. The wall at the back of the built-in burners is made of sea shells. The model is Joyce Donnell, Norman. Staff Photo. Published July 6, 1957, *THE DAILY OKLAHOMAN*.

Page 105
Rock and Roll fans are getting their big time at the Exposition as bands from coast to coast spell popular Oklahoma area disc jockeys in the huge pavilion of Teen-Town, U.S.A. The fully chaperoned dance area is surrounded by teen-age shops and milk bars. Staff Photo by Dick Cobb. Published June 16, 1957, *THE DAILY OKLAHOMAN*.

CHAPTER FOUR
LINES IN THE SAND

Page 106
A night time view of downtown Oklahoma City looking northwest from the Crosstown Expressway, January, 1995. Staff Photo by Jim Argo. *THE OKLAHOMAN COLLECTION*. Unpublished.

Page 107
"Flower child" appears impassive as she listens Saturday to speeches denouncing the U.S. role in the Vietnam conflict during a peace demonstration on the University of Oklahoma campus in Norman. Staff Photo by Jim Argo. Published Apr. 13, 1969, *THE DAILY OKLAHOMAN*.

Page 108
These demonstrators wrote notes to those outside. Staff Photo by George Tapscott. Published May 31, 1963, *OKLAHOMA CITY TIMES*.

Page 109 (left)
Young demonstrators standing in front of Bishops Restaurant in downtown Oklahoma City, June 4, 1963. Staff Photo by Mandell Matheson. *THE OKLAHOMAN COLLECTION*. Unpublished.

Page 109 (center)
Racial demonstrators leave church after rally. Staff Photo by John Gumm. Published Aug. 19, 1961, *OKLAHOMA CITY TIMES*.

Page 109 (right)
Dr. E.C. Snow, Jr., left, and unidentified companion picket stores on W. Main. Staff Photo by Dick Cobb. Published Aug. 22, 1960, *OKLAHOMA CITY TIMES*.

BIOS FOR OKLAHOMA
NASA ASTRONAUTS

Page 110 (left)
Stuart A. Roosa, Air Force Colonel, attended school in Claremore and then Oklahoma State University. He became an astronaut in 1966 and was a member of the Apollo 14 crew that flew Jan. 31 to Feb. 9, 1971. *NASA Photo/THE OKLAHOMAN COLLECTION*.

Page 110 (right)
Leroy Gordon Cooper, Jr., was selected as an astronaut in 1959 and flew on Mercury 9, May 15-16, 1963, and on Gemini 5, Aug. 21 to Aug. 29, 1965. Born in Shawnee on Mar. 6, 1927, Cooper retired as a colonel from the U.S. Air Force. *NASA Photo/THE OKLAHOMAN COLLECTION*.

Page 111 (top left)
William R. Pogue was selected for the astronaut program in 1966 and flew on Skylab 4, Nov. 16, 1973, to Feb. 8, 1974. Born in Okemah on Jan. 23, 1930, Pogue retired as a colonel from the U.S. Air Force. *NASA Photo/THE OKLAHOMAN COLLECTION*.

Page 111 (bottom left)
Owen K. Garriott was selected as an astronaut in 1959 and flew on Mercury 9, May 15-16, 1963, and STS-9 Nov. 28 to Dec. 8, 1983. Born in Enid on Nov. 22, 1930, Garriott entered the program as a civilian. *NASA Photo/ THE OKLAHOMAN COLLECTION*.

Page 111 (center)
Astronaut Thomas P. Stafford, fomer Oklahoman from Weatherford, and Eugene Cernan wave to the crowd during a parade (in downtown Oklahoma City.) Staff Photo by Jim Argo. Published July 8, 1966, *OKLAHOMA CITY TIMES*.

Page 111 (center)
Thomas P. Stafford was selected for the astronaut program in 1962 and flew on Gemini 6, Dec. 15-16, 1965; Gemini 9, June 3-6, 1966; Apollo 10, May 18-26, 1969, and the Apollo-Soyuz Test Project, July 15-24, 1975. Born in Weatherford Sept. 17, 1930, Stafford retired as a lieutenant general from the U.S. Air Force.

Page 111 (top right)
Shannon W. Lucid, a civilian, was born in China on Jan. 14, 1943, to missionary parents but was reared in Bethany. She was selected by NASA for the astronaut program in 1973 and was a member of the Discovery mission of 1985, Atlantis, 1991 and Columbia mission of 1993. She currently holds the United States single mission space flight endurance record on the Space Station Mir. This mission began Mar. 22, 1996, and ended Sept. 26, 1996. She traveled 75.2 million miles in 188 days, 4 hours and 14 seconds. *NASA Photo/THE OKLAHOMAN COLLECTION.*

Page 112
Trustees of the Cowboy Hall of Fame inspect the partially finished structure in Oklahoma City. Staff Photo by Bob Albright. Published Sept. 11, 1968, *THE DAILY OKLAHOMAN.*

Page 113 (left)
A packed State Fair Arena awaits ready rider (during the National Finals Rodeo). Staff Photo by Jim Argo. Published Dec. 10, 1976, *OKLAHOMA CITY TIMES.*

Page 113 (top right)
Jack Lemmon and Glenn Ford, stars of "Cowboy," get together with a real champ in the boots and saddle department. Jim Shoulders (center), three times world champion cowboy, was also honored at Columbia Pictures' chuck wagon feed held Tuesday prior to the world premiere of the movie. George Chyka Productions/*THE OKLAHOMAN COLLECTION.* Published Jan. 12, 1958, *THE DAILY OKLAHOMAN.*

Page 113 (bottom right)
Bull riders have their ups and downs. Marvin Shoulders seems in command and does stay atop Sonny Boy Thursday to maintain his lead in the National Finals Rodeo competition. The Henryetta cowboy is the only bull rider

to stay atop all of his six bulls the required eight seconds in the Finals. Staff Photo by Roger Artman. Published Dec. 12, 1973, *OKLAHOMA CITY TIMES.*

Page 114
Webbers Falls lock and dam will reach three-fourths of a mile across the Arkansas (River) between two high bluffs. It extends waterway 37 miles to Lock 17. Photo by Tulsa District, Corps of Engineers/THE OKLAHOMAN COLLECTION. Published Dec. 29, 1967, *OKLAHOMA CITY TIMES.*

Page 115 (left)
SEVERAL MONTHS of work remain before lock and dam No. 17 southeast of Wagoner is ready for operation. Located 368.8 miles upstream on the Arkansas River Navigation System it is expected to be ready for use by fall. Staff Aerial Photo by Al McLaughlin. Published Apr. 19, 1970, *THE DAILY OKLAHOMAN.*

Page 115 (top right)
Chief executive (President Richard M. Nixon) lauds Oklahomans' progress against a backdrop of vessels anchored on the Verdigris River to symbolize its use. Staff Photo by Jim Argo. Published June 6, 1971, *THE DAILY OKLAHOMAN.*

Page 115 (bottom right)
Largest eight barge tow to ever enter at Robert S. Kerr lock and dam on the Arkansas River, December, 1974. *THE OKLAHOMAN COLLECTION.* Unpublished.

Page 116 (top left)
Leaving OSU football field, ROTC cadets march through crowd of protestors following peaceful demonstration. Staff Photo by Joe Aker. Published May 8, 1970, *THE DAILY OKLAHOMAN.*

Page 116 (bottom left)
Three OSU students appeared at a gathering of antiwar protestors Thursday at Oklahoma State University carrying this U.S. Flag. They said they were "for the United States" and took

turns holding the flag in a brisk wind. Staff Photo by Joe Aker. Published May 8, 1970, *OKLAHOMA CITY TIMES.*

Page 116 (right)
A huge crowd of students demonstrates in front of the Edmon Low Library on the campus of Oklahoma State University, Stillwater, Nov. 8, 1967. Staff Photo by Austin Traverse. *THE OKLAHOMAN COLLECTION.* Unpublished.

Page 117 (left)
An unidentified protestor waves a small American flag while protesting ROTC parade at the University of Oklahoma in Norman May 13, 1970. Staff Photo by Jim Argo. *THE OKLAHOMAN COLLECTION.* Unpublished

Page 117 (top right)
Students watch combined ROTC Awards Review at the University of Oklahoma Tuesday. Staff Photo by Jim Argo. Published May 13, 1970, *THE DAILY OKLAHOMAN.*

Page 117 (bottom right)
Riot batons at the ready, highway patrol troopers confront students blocking a police vehicle during uproar on the University of Oklahoma campus Tuesday afternoon. Officers finally used clubs to reach the car. The incident developed after some students began an anti-ROTC demonstration. Staff Photo. Published May 6, 1970, *OKLAHOMA CITY TIMES.*

Page 118 (left)
Cecil Williams confronts Oklahoma City police officers during the city's sanitation workers strike Aug. 21, 1969. Staff Photo by Jim Argo. *THE OKLAHOMAN COLLECTION.* Unpublished.

Page 118 (center)
Protesting her arrest at Westward garage, Mrs. Clara Luper is led away by Officer John Felled. Staff Photo by Jim Argo. Published Aug. 21, 1969, *OKLAHOMA CITY TIMES.*

Page 118 (right)
Still reading from the Bible, the Rev. W.K. Jackson is carried by police from in front of a city garbage truck. Staff Photo by Tony Wood. Published Oct. 24, 1969, *OKLAHOMA CITY TIMES.*

Page 119
Douglass High School demonstrators march across Hudson this afternoon on their way west on Park Ave. to city hall. Staff Photo by George Tapscott. Published Oct. 30, 1969, *OKLAHOMA CITY TIMES.*

Page 120 (left)
White students cluster around street corner outside Southeast High School following disturbances. The sign shows their dislike for the Finger desegregation plan. Staff Photo by Jim Argo. Published Sept. 1, 1972, *THE DAILY OKLAHOMAN.*

Page 120 (right)
A young teenager carries a protest sign during an anti-busing rally in Oklahoma City in this Aug. 29, 1972, photo. Staff Photo by J. Pat Carter. *THE OKLAHOMAN COLLECTION.* Unpublished.

Page 121
Striking blows against the involuntary busing of Oklahoma school children and present and future school integration plans, Councilman John Smith led a "bus bash" Saturday where adults and children, armed with sledgehammers, hammers and axes wrecked a school bus. Windows went first, then the headlights and top as youngsters punched holes in the roof and parents pounded away at the sides of the bus Smith bought and placed at SE 74 and Shields. Staff Photo by Jim Argo. Published Feb. 22, 1970, *THE DAILY OKLAHOMAN.*

Page 122 (top left)
Under arrest, black students gesture from a police paddy wagon at Southeast High School as officers quell fighting at the racially troubled south side school. At least eleven students

were arrested during an outbreak of violence this morning and several injuries were reported. Staff Photo by Jim Argo. Published Aug. 31, 1972, OKLAHOMA CITY TIMES.

Page 122 (right)
FRIENDS RESTRAIN this young girl whose anguish-ridden features convey the frustration felt by many youths during the troubles that erupted at Southeast High School Thursday morning. Staff Photo by Jim Argo. Published Sept. 1, 1972, THE DAILY OKLAHOMAN.

Page 123
Policeman struggles with a youth during a racial disturbance today at Southeast High School. Staff Photo by Jim Argo. Published Aug. 31, 1972, OKLAHOMA CITY TIMES.

Page 124
Smoke billows from a number of buildings in the industrial area of Oklahoma State Penitentiary early in riot Friday. Staff Aerial Photo by Al McLaughlin. Published July 28, 1973, THE DAILY OKLAHOMAN.

Page 125 (left)
Inmates wait Monday for a cell block shakedown to be completed. Two in this group (the second from the left and the second from the right) carry knives partially hidden by their clothing. Some inmates say they did not participate in the riot and carry weapons because they fear reprisals from those who did. These men are outside the main prison walls, but behind a tall chain link fence. Staff Photo by Jim Argo. Published July 31, 1973, THE DAILY OKLAHOMAN.

Page 125 (top right)
Oklahoma Highway Patrolmen take a break during the Oklahoma State Penitentiary riot on July 28, 1973. Staff Photo. THE OKLAHOMAN COLLECTION. Unpublished.

Page 125 (bottom right)
A damaged cell block during the July 28, 1973, prison riot at the Oklahoma State Penitentiary

in McAlester. Staff Photo by Jim Argo. THE OKLAHOMAN COLLECTION. Unpublished.

Page 126 (left)
A Viking war ship, a huge Mexican hat and a swimming pool were among the entries shoving off from Sand Springs Monday during the three-hour launching of the Seventh Annual Great Raft Race down the Arkansas River to Tulsa. Among the 3,500 participants were Gov. George Nigh and his wife Donna. Winners of the event, sponsored by a Tulsa radio station, will be announced later. Staff Photo. Published Sept. 4, 1979, THE DAILY OKLAHOMAN.

Page 126 (right)
Practicing while awaiting their turn on the fiddlers' platform are Jim Brunson and Paula Brunson, both of Conway, Ark. They were among 15 fiddlers participating in the Seventh Annual Hugo Bluegrass Festival held this past weekend. Staff Photo by Jim Argo. Published Aug. 10, 1975, THE DAILY OKLAHOMAN.

Page 127
Watermelon is enjoyed by people of all ages (at the Rush Springs Watermelon Festival) as witnessed by from left, Jeff Haynes, 6, Rush Springs; Stella Powers, Oklahoma City, and Jeff's brother Doyle, 9. Staff Photo by Gary Guidice. Published Aug. 11, 1974, THE DAILY OKLAHOMAN.

Page 128
PUBLIC EVACUATION test of a supersonic transport Thursday at Oklahoma City's Federal Aviation Administration facility saw 289 persons pouring out of emergency exits in two separate tests to determine future construction safety standards. Staff Photo by Bob Albright. Published Nov. 11, 1967, THE DAILY OKLAHOMAN.

Page 129 (left)
Passengers in the Federal Aviation Administration's evacuation simulator leap into an emergency escape chute during a timed test.

Staff Photo by Joe Wilson. Published Oct. 16, 1971, THE DAILY OKLAHOMAN.

Page 129 (top right)
Jumping into a swimming pool as part of the day's work might sound like fun. At the Civil Aeromedical Research Institute it's serious business, however. Research is under way at present to determine the most effective way for crew members to leave a cargo plane, which might ditch in the ocean. Staff Photo by Jim Argo. Published Sept. 17, 1964, OKLAHOMA CITY TIMES.

Page 129 (bottom right)
MEN FROM MARS? Not exactly, but that is what it looks like. Twenty persons are attending a course at the Federal Aviation Agency on high altitude flight and how to cope with it. The oxygen masks give them this weird Halloween look. Higher flying general aviation aircraft prompted the FAA to offer the course. Staff Photo by Jim Argo. Published Oct. 31, 1964, OKLAHOMA CITY TIMES.

Page 130
THE FINAL ACT is a solo performance for the torn and tattered stage of the Midwest Theater, once a first-class downtown movie hall. The rest of the building, including the nine-story office building that was its west entrance, has been torn down to make way for the retail Galleria. Urban Renewal spokesman Jack Bagby said the stage will probably meet its fate in a couple of weeks. Staff Photo by Paul Southerland. Published June 18, 1976, THE DAILY OKLAHOMAN.

Page 131 (left)
Three young people comfortably seated on the hood of their car were among many who turned out Sunday morning to witness the nondemolition of the Biltmore Hotel. Staff Photo by Monty Reed. Published Sept. 12, 1977, THE DAILY OKLAHOMAN.

Page 131 (center)
The 26 story Biltmore Hotel, built in 1932, was demolished to make way for an urban renewal project. At the time it was the tallest steel-reinforced building in the world ever demolished with explosives. Nine hundred explosive charges were used in the building to bring it down, in this picture dated Oct. 16, 1977. Staff Photo by Paul Southerland. THE OKLAHOMAN COLLECTION. Unpublished

Page 131 (right)
Craning their necks at the crane, spectators–state legislators, and city officials among them—watch downtown urban renewal demolition. Staff Photo by Bob Albright. Published Mar. 30, 1968, OKLAHOMA CITY TIMES.

CHAPTER FIVE
COMING TOGETHER

Page 132
The 1980's brought a major change in downtown Oklahoma City with the construction of the Myriad Botanical Gardens and Crystal Bridge Tropical Conservatory. Staff Photo by Jim Argo taken August, 1982. THE OKLAHOMAN COLLECTION. Unpublished.

Page 133
A statue titled "Welcome Sundown" by artist Hollis Williford stands in front of the National Cowboy Hall of Fame and Western Heritage Center in Oklahoma City. Staff Photo by Jim Argo. Published Apr. 23, 1995, THE SUNDAY OKLAHOMAN.

Page 134 (left)
Scott Beard of El Reno stakes his claim during a "land run" in Guthrie Saturday morning. During the 1889 Land Run, settlers came by horse and train to find a homestead in the Unassigned Lands. Staff Photo by Jim Argo. Published Apr. 23, 1989, THE SUNDAY OKLAHOMAN.

Page 134 (right)
Placing the Statue: Workers lower the Cherokee Strip Centennial statue onto its base Tuesday in Ponca City. The statue, formerly titled "This Land Is Mine," raised a stir among some American Indians who said the name overlooked the fact that the land claimed by Cherokee Strip settlers had belonged to Indians. Staff Photo by Jim Argo, Sept. 8, 1993. THE OKLAHOMAN COLLECTION. Unpublished.

Page 135
A super wide-angle lens presents an interesting view Thursday of "Hopes and Dreams" as it's unveiled on the Noble County Court House lawn. Staff Photo by Jim Argo. Published Sept. 17, 1973, THE DAILY OKLAHOMAN.

Page 136 (left)
The landscape within a mile of his home in Apache has been inspiration enough for Doc Tate Nevaquaya. Breaks from his painting frequently entail a conversation between him and his flute in this outdoor spot. On Wednesday, he will be named a State Treasure by the State Arts Council. Staff Photo by Jim Argo. Published Oct. 8, 1995, THE SUNDAY OKLAHOMAN.

Page 136 (right)
The Cimarron Valley Railroad Museum is a private venture of Bob Read, Jr. and Bob Read, Sr. who saved the Yale depot and took it home with them. All the dogs that hang around the station are named after Santa Fe engines. Staff Photo by Jim Argo. Published Sept. 27, 1992, THE SUNDAY OKLAHOMAN.

Page 137
Master builder, Luke Robison and a crew of volunteers spent months restoring the historic round barn in Arcadia, only to have the dome shaped roof collapse. The crane, on loan from a local company as a donation, is being used to help suspend rafters for the barn's new roof. Staff Photo by Jim Beckel. Aug. 10, 1990, THE OKLAHOMAN COLLECTION. Unpublished.

Page 138 (top left)
Route 66 Museum curator Pat Smith and her husband Virgil treat Koralyn, 7, and Cody, 3, Mixon to a Moon Pie inside a restored diner recently added to the (Route 66) museum's collection (in Clinton), in this July 2, 2003, photo. Staff Photo by Steve Sisney. THE OKLAHOMAN COLLECTION. Unpublished.

Page 138 (bottom left)
TOURISTS STILL GET THEIR KICKS; The Route 66 Museum in Clinton is the Oklahoma Historical Society's answer to a still-growing interest in the old Mother Road. The highway draws tourists from across the nation and several European and Asian countries. Staff Photo by Jim Argo. Published Apr. 26, 1998, THE SUNDAY OKLAHOMAN.

Page 138 (right)
A 1956 Plymouth Belvedere (in the Route 66 Museum in Elk City) might have been seen outside any of the diners beside Route 66. Staff Photo by David McDaniel. Published Feb. 28, 2002, THE DAILY OKLAHOMAN.

Page 139 (left)
Gardens at Tulsa's Philbrook Museum of Art will soon undergo a multi-million-dollar facelift. Oklahoma Tourism Department Photo by Fred W. Marvel. Published May 23, 2002, THE DAILY OKLAHOMAN.

Page 139 (right)
The collection of western art in (Tulsa's) Gilcrease includes 57 Frederic Remingtons, 88 Charles M. Russells, 81 Willard Stones and hundreds of works by other respected artists. Staff Photo by David McDaniel. Published Nov. 27, 1994, THE SUNDAY OKLAHOMAN.

Page 140 (left)
A pufferfish appears to be staring at something at the Oklahoma Aquarium (in Jenks). Staff Photo by Paul Hellstern. Published May 25, 2003, THE DAILY OKLAHOMAN.

Page 140 (right)
An Imperial mammoth is poised Monday to take its place in the rotunda of the Sam Noble Oklahoma Museum of Natural History in Norman. After days of maneuvering the 5,000-pound bronze statue into the building, museum workers on Monday bolted the work into place. Staff Photo by Jaconna Aguirre. Published Jan. 11, 2000, THE DAILY OKLAHOMAN.

Page 141 (left)
Oklahoma City Museum of Art Executive Director Carolyn Hill was on hand Tuesday when the lights came on for the Eleanor Blake Kirkpatrick Memorial Tower, a blown glass sculpture by Seattle artist Dale Chihuly. Commissioned for the museum in memory of the late art patron Kirkpatrick, the 55-foot tower is Chihuly's largest artwork. A three-story glass atrium offers a view from inside or outside the downtown museum. Admission to the $22.5 million building is free during the museum's public opening Saturday and Sunday. Staff Photo by Steve Sisney. Published Mar. 13, 2002, THE DAILY OKLAHOMAN.

Page 141 (right)
Roofers inspect sheet metal sections of the new Oklahoma Historical Society offices (and History Center Museum) under construction north of the state Capitol near NE 23 and Lincoln Boulevard in this Jan. 22, 2004, photo. Staff Photo by Paul B. Southerland. THE OKLAHOMAN COLLECTION. Unpublished.

Page 142
University of Oklahoma football coaches Merv Johnson and Barry Switzer here direct action from the sidelines during a game, which led the Sooner football team back to the Orange Bowl in the 1985 season. Staff Photo. THE OKLAHOMAN COLLECTION. Unpublished.

Page 143 (left)
Oklahoma State University coach Eddie Sutton cuts down the net after winning the Big 12 Basketball Tournament in Dallas, Tex. Staff

Photo by Bryan Terry. Published Mar. 14, 2004, NEWSOK.COM.

Page 143 (right)
University of Oklahoma coach Bob Stoops helps his team hold up the Big 12 Championship trophy after their big win in Kansas City on Saturday. Staff Photo by Bryan Terry. Published Dec. 5, 2004, THE OKLAHOMAN.

Page 144
Apr. 19, 1995, became the morning of terror as a rental truck loaded with explosives was detonated in front of the Alfred P. Murrah Federal Building in downtown Oklahoma City. Staff Photo by Jim Argo. THE OKLAHOMAN COLLECTION. Unpublished.

Page 145 (left)
Injured workers and children from the Downtown YMCA Child Development Center wait for rescue, comforting injured children. Staff Photo by Steve Gooch. Apr. 19, 1995, THE OKLAHOMAN COLLECTION. Unpublished.

Page 145 (right)
An Oklahoma County sheriff's deputy assists with an injured infant. Staff Photo by Steve Gooch. Published Apr. 20, 1995, THE DAILY OKLAHOMAN.

Page 146
Rescue workers gather on the third floor of the federal building to work on gaining access to the day care center that was located on the second floor. Huge cranes used in the search and rescue operation loom outside the shattered structure. Staff Photo by David McDaniel. Published Apr. 25, 1995, THE DAILY OKLAHOMAN.

Page 147 (left)
An unidentified rescue worker places flowers in front of the damaged building in this Apr. 27, 1995, photo. Staff Photo by Jim Argo. THE OKLAHOMAN COLLECTION. Unpublished.

Page 147 (top right)
A media "satellite city" sprang up downtown in the aftermath of the explosion at the Alfred P. Murrah Federal Building. Staff Photo by Paul Hellstern. Published Apr. 23, 1995, *THE SUNDAY OKLAHOMAN.*

Page 147 (bottom right)
Honoring the victims of the Murrah building bombing Sunday, Hillary and President Clinton and Cathy and Gov. Frank Keating stand next to Jason Smith and Dan McKinney, son and husband of Secret Service Agent Laura McKinney. She was in the federal building when it was bombed and was still missing. Staff Photo by Jim Argo. Published Apr. 24, 1995, *THE DAILY OKLAHOMAN.*

Page 148
A visitor to the fence looks at the teddy bears tied to a chain link fence as a reminder of the 168 victims of the bombing in this Apr. 22, 1995, photo. Staff Photo by Jim Beckel. *THE OKLAHOMAN COLLECTION.* Unpublished.

Page 149 (top)
Photo taken by a remote camera from the Journal Record Building looking south. Staff Photo by George R. Wilson. Published Apr. 24, 1995, *THE DAILY OKLAHOMAN.*

Page 149 (bottom left)
Glenn Wilburn hugs his weeping wife, Kathy, as they and their daughter, Edye Smith, watch Tuesday's destruction of the federal building where Smith's two sons, Chase, 3, and Colton, 2, died April 19. Staff Photo by Paul B. Southerland. Published May 24, 1995, *THE DAILY OKLAHOMAN.*

Page 150 (left)
Families and friends gather beneath the Survivor Tree after the dedication of the Oklahoma City National Memorial. Staff Photo by David McDaniel. Published Apr. 19, 2000, *NEWSOK. COM.*

Page 150 (right)
President Clinton dips a finger in the reflecting pool at the center of the memorial. Staff Photo by David McDaniel. Published Apr. 20, 2000, *THE DAILY OKLAHOMAN.*

Page 151 (left)
Relatives of Kathy Lynn Seidl, a Secret Service employee who died in the 1995 bombing, join hands around her chair during a private dedication ceremony Wednesday morning at the Oklahoma City National Memorial. Staff Photo by Bryan Terry. Published Apr. 20, 2000, *THE DAILY OKLAHOMAN.*

Page 151 (top right)
President Bush and Roberto Martinez, a family member of one of the bombing victims, embrace during the dedication (of the Oklahoma City National Memorial Center Museum). Staff Photo by Jim Beckel. Published Feb. 20, 2001, *THE DAILY OKLAHOMAN.*

Page 151 (bottom right)
Don Ferrell, who lost a daughter, Susan, in the bombing, reads "Messages from the Generations" during the museum's dedication. Staff Photo by David McDaniel. Published Feb. 19, 2001, *NEWSOK.COM.*

Page 152 (left)
Dorothy J. Faulkner of Oklahoma City holds a Martin Luther King Jr. poster in the crowd Monday at the Oklahoma Historical Society during the King Holiday bell-ringing. (In the background, Clara Luper speaks to the crowd.) Staff Photo by Paul B. Southerland. Published Jan. 20, 2004, *THE OKLAHOMAN.*

Page 152 (right)
Isaac Hamilton, 8, of Tulsa, patiently waits for a performance during the 40th annual Sac and Fox Powwow south of Stroud. The dances continue through Sunday. Staff Photo by Bryan Terry. Published July 12, 2003, *THE DAILY OKLAHOMAN.*

Page 153 (left)
Anna Dinh performs a traditional Vietnamese Hat Dance at the Moon Festival. Staff Photo by Michael Downes. Published Sept. 15, 2003, *THE DAILY OKLAHOMAN.*

Page 153 (center)
Shani Kim, 5, receives last-minute lipstick from her mother, Sophia Kim, before Shani's performance in the Doll Dance during the Asian Festival at the Myriad Gardens on Saturday. Staff Photo by Doug Hoke. Published May 20, 2003, *THE DAILY OKLAHOMAN.*

Page 153 (right)
Jose Munoz, a member of the Awiratzi Mexican Folkloric Dance Company, performs a Mexican dance Wednesday for students at Putnam City's Apollo Elementary School. Munoz and other dancers visited the school to help students celebrate Cinco de Mayo. Staff Photo by Steve Gooch. Published May 6, 2004, *THE OKLAHOMAN.*

Page 154
Workers are finishing steel work at the new Bricktown ball park, with masonry and flooring installation scheduled to start sometime in the next couple of weeks. The ballpark, funded by the $300 million Metropolitan Area Projects plan, is to open in 1998. Staff Photo by David McDaniel. Published Mar. 23, 1997, *THE DAILY OKLAHOMAN.*

Page 155 (left)
A statue of baseball great Mickey Mantle looms over the crowd gathered Thursday outside the Southwestern Bell Bricktown Ballpark in downtown Oklahoma City. The sculpture was dedicated as part of the celebration officially opening the new home of the Oklahoma RedHawks. Staff Photo by Steve Gooch. Published Apr. 17, 1998, *THE DAILY OKLAHOMAN.*

Page 155 (right)
Baseball returned to downtown Oklahoma City on Thursday night when the Oklahoma Red-Hawks opened Southwestern Bell Bricktown Ballpark with a 6-3 loss to the Edmonton Trappers. Staff Photo by Amy Kennedy. Published Apr. 17, 1998, *THE DAILY OKLAHOMAN.*

Page 156 (left)
Passengers ride a water taxi Friday on the Bricktown canal shortly after the lighting of The Oklahoman Christmas Tree. The tree, shown in the background, was lit by Mayor Mick Cornett across the street from the SBC Bricktown Ballpark in downtown Oklahoma City. Staff Photo by Steve Sisney. Published Nov. 27, 2004, *THE OKLAHOMAN.*

Page 156 (right)
Riders on a canal boat in Bricktown use hats and umbrellas Wednesday to block the sun's rays. Warm, breezy weather will be the story in Oklahoma for the coming days, forecasters say. The National Weather Service said skies will be mostly sunny today, with a slight chance for thunderstorms in southeastern Oklahoma. Staff Photo by Bryan Terry. Published June 20, 2002, *THE DAILY OKLAHOMAN.*

Page 157 (left)
Wynton Marsalis waits on stage Thursday night to play as part of the activities celebrating the reopening of the Civic Center Music Hall. He is one of many performers taking part in the celebration that runs through Sunday. Staff Photo by Bryan Terry. Published Sept. 7, 2001, *THE DAILY OKLAHOMAN.*

Page 157 (right)
Local high school students position their boat during rowing practice at the Chesapeake Bay area off the Canadian River. Some of the students have received college scholarships in rowing. Staff Photo by Bryan Terry. Published Feb. 19, 2003, *THE DAILY OKLAHOMAN.*

Page 158
The crowd gathers Friday night in the three rings before the start of the Ringling Bros. and Barnum & Bailey Circus, the first event held at the new Ford Center. The Ringling Bros. circus is making its first stop in Oklahoma City since 1997. The remaining shows are 11:30 a.m., 3:30 and 7:30 p.m. today, and 1:30 and 5:30 p.m. Sunday. Staff Photo by Bryan Terry. Published June 15, 2002. *THE DAILY OKLAHOMAN.*

Page 159.
Tom Ellis of Midwest City, left, passes a book to Jenny Fenner, Oklahoma City, as part of Friday's ceremonial book passing, one of the festivities heralding Tuesday's grand opening of the Ronald J. Norick Downtown Library at 300 Park Ave. Staff Photo by David McDaniel. Published Aug. 14, 2004, *THE OKLAHOMAN.*

Page 160
The deadly (F5) tornado is shown in the above photo crossing Pennsylvania Avenue near SW 134, where scores of homes were damaged and destroyed Monday evening. Staff Photo by Paul Hellstern. Published May 4, 1999, *THE DAILY OKLAHOMAN.*

Page 161 (left)
Rescuers help Renee Faulkinberry out from under the rubble of her home in Country Place Estates in southwest Oklahoma City. Staff Photo by Paul Hellstern. Published May 4, 1999, *THE DAILY OKLAHOMAN.*

Page 161 (right)
Rescue workers load victims into ambulances near Westmoore High School on Monday night in south Oklahoma City. Staff Photo by Steve Sisney. Published May 4, 1999, *THE DAILY OKLAHOMAN.*

Page 162
An aerial view of Moore shows the massive damage path left by Monday's tornado. Police say that half of the city's 15,000 homes were damaged or destroyed by the killer storm while thousands have been left homeless or without power. First Baptist Church, which sustained minor damage, can be seen at the top right.

Staff Photo by Paul Hellstern. Published May 5, 1999, *THE DAILY OKLAHOMAN.*

Page 163 (left)
Camile Melton holds her daughter Hannah, 5, and takes part in the worship service Sunday of the Ridgecrest Baptist Church (in Bridge Creek). Staff Photo by Paul Hellstern. Published May 10, 1999, *THE DAILY OKLAHOMAN.*

Page 163 (top right)
Al Fronko sits Friday in front of his home in Moore that was destroyed by Thursday night's tornado. Franko's garage occupied the space to his right. Hundreds of Oklahomans spent Friday beginning to clean up what was left of their homes. Staff Photo by Ty Russell. Published May 10, 2003, *THE DAILY OKLAHOMAN.*

Page 163 (bottom right)
Lawrence Bishop, center, interim pastor of Stroud's First Christian Church, talks to Thelma Maulding-McCammon as H.B. McCammon stands in the kitchen of the roofless house. Monday was the third time the home had been hit by a tornado since H.B. McCammon, 82, has lived there. Staff Photo by Steve Sisney. Published May 5, 1999, *THE DAILY OKLAHOMAN.*

Page 164
Capt. Steven Mason of El Centro, Calif, guides the refueling boom of a KC-135 Stratotanker from Altus Air Force Base as it refuels the Thunderbirds jets Thursday. Staff Photo by Steve Sisney. Published Apr. 28, 2000, *THE DAILY OKLAHOMAN.*

Page 165
An officer, standing inside a hangar, is silhouetted against an E-3A airplane as he salutes during a change-of-command ceremony for the 552nd Air Control Wing at Tinker AFB Tuesday morning. Staff Photo by Jim Beckel. Published May 8, 2004, *THE OKLAHOMAN.*

Page 166
The crew of Nabors 622 places a cement pour head on a well owned by Chesapeake Energy Corp. in the natural gas fields near Marlow, Oct. 21, 2004. Staff Photo by Steve Sisney. *THE OKLAHOMAN COLLECTION.* Unpublished.

Page 167 (left)
Dozens of wind turbines, as tall as 20-story buildings, are going up in Western Oklahoma among the cattle, salt cedar, sagebrush and gypsum rock. Copyright photo by josephmills.com. Published July 18, 2003, *THE DAILY OKLAHOMAN.*

Page 167 (right)
Construction crews appear miniature compared with the size of the foundation they are readying for a wind turbine. A wind turbine's foundation must support a 20-story tower. Copyright photo by josephmills.com. Published July 18, 2003, *THE DAILY OKLAHOMAN.*

Page 168 (left)
Ken and Marrin York, Ponca City, along with their two sons Nathan and Sean search for a family Christmas tree at Santa's Forest Christmas tree farm west of town. Staff Photo by Jim Argo. Dec. 12, 1998, *THE OKLAHOMAN COLLECTION.* Unpublished.

Page 168 (right)
Mary and John Konwerski of Tecumseh sample some wine Saturday afternoon at the Art and Wine festival. Oklahoma just passed a law allowing wine by the glass at wine festivals. Staff Photo by Jaconna Aguirre. June 12, 2004, *THE OKLAHOMAN COLLECTION.* Unpublished.

Page 169
Gordon Couch uses a tree shaker at his family-owned pecan orchard near Luther, Okla. Staff Photo by Steve Sisney. Published Nov. 21, 2001, *THE DAILY OKLAHOMAN.*

Page 170 (left)
William and Donna Stacy, McLoud, add their names to a beam that will be part of the new state Capitol dome, June 19, 2001. Staff Photo by Steve Sisney. *THE OKLAHOMAN COLLECTION.* Unpublished.

Page 170 (right)
Kristen Richardson, 6, of Oklahoma City adds her name Tuesday to a beam that will help support the dome being built on top of the state Capitol. Gov. Frank Keating and several lawmakers are going to have a "skybreaking" ceremony at 10 a.m. today. Staff Photo by Steve Sisney. Published June 20, 2001, *THE DAILY OKLAHOMAN.*

Page 171 (left)
State Sen. Kelly Haney, D-Seminole, adds clay to the face of a statue of an American Indian on Friday. With the legislative session now over, the politician, a Seminole-Creek, can devote his time to the sculpture. The work will be put atop the state Capitol dome. Staff Photo by Jim Beckel. Published June 2, 2001, *THE DAILY OKLAHOMAN.*

Page 171 (right)
Bill Anderson walks along the buttress level of the (state Capitol) dome. Staff Photo by Steve Sisney. Published Apr. 13, 2002. *THE DAILY OKLAHOMAN.*

Page 172
Fireworks explode over the state Capitol as part of Saturday's dedication of the dome. Staff Photo by Bryan Terry. Published Nov. 17, 2002, *THE SUNDAY OKLAHOMAN.*

Page 173 (left)
Opera star, Leona Mitchell sings the National Anthem during the Oklahoma State Capitol dome dedication. Staff Photo by Ty Russell. Published Nov. 16, 2002, *NEWSOK.COM.*

Page 173 (top right)
Former Miss Americas from Oklahoma; Shawn-
tel Smith-Wuerch, left, Jane Jayroe, center and
Susan Powell sing at the dedication ceremony.
Staff Photo by Ty Russell. Published Nov. 16,
2002, *NEWSOK.COM.*

Page 173 (bottom right)
Vince Gill, the master of ceremonies for the
dome dedication, sings a song Saturday night.
Staff Photo by Ty Russell. Published Nov. 17,
2002, *THE DAILY OKLAHOMAN.*

OUR STORY

Page 174
Oklahoma's new Capitol dome shows off its
colorful interior splendor in this 2002 photograph. Staff Photo by Steve Sisney. *THE
OKLAHOMAN COLLECTION.* Unpublished.

Page 175
The 17-foot-tall statue of "The Guardian," by
artist Kelly Haney, atop the Oklahoma Capitol
dome. Copyright photo by Hugh Scott.

STAFF PHOTOGRAPHERS

The first group of staff photographers in the 1930s were true pioneers in newspaper photography. During the next seven decades, 87 photographers, both men and women provided newspaper readers the visual image of the story. News photographers became photojournalists. Their equipment, the standard 4x5 Speed Graf-lex during the 1930s through the 1950s, gave way to small cameras and better lenses. Today's photographers use a digital camera that records the image on a memory card instead of film. This book is a tribute to all photographers in Oklahoma who have recorded, in photographs, the state's history.

1920s
Alvin C. Rucker
    Photographer/reporter

1930s
Gerry Allred
Alphia Hart
C.J. Kaho
Clyde Mapes
A.Y. Owen
Ron Pyer
Wm. 'Bill' Shroder Jr.
George Tapscott
Bennie Turner

1940s
Betty Baughman
Bill Brookes
Robin Broun
Bill Burns
George Cauthen
Dick Cobb
Bob East
Charles Hamm
Bill Johnson
Tom Killian
Jim Lucas

Al McLaughlin
Richard Meeks
Joe Miller
Morris Sparlin
Bill Stockwell
Gene Thomas
John Turner

1950s
Bob Albright
John Gumm
Bob Hauton
    Photographer/reporter
Cliff King
Richard Peterson
Kazimir (Casey) Petraus-kas
James Swatek*
Austin Traverse

1960s
Jim Argo
Don Brown
Ray Foster
Bob Heaton
Ron Hill

Mandell Matheson
Hank Mooney
Tony Wood

1970s
Joe Aker
Roger Artman*
J.Pat Carter
Randy Carter*
J. Don Cook
Paul Derby
Bob Etheridge
Bob Grier
Gary Guidice
Dave Heaton*
Doug Hoke
Roger Klock
Larry Maloney
David McDaniel
Monty Reed*
Paul B. Southerland
Michal Thompson*
Cliff Traverse
Don Tullous
Bob Vahlberg*
Joe Wilson

1980s
Jim Beckel
Jeff Buehner*
Roberta Burnett*
David Faytinger*
Steve Gooch
Paul Hellstern
Paul S. Howell
David Longstreath*
Renee Lynn*
Steve Sisney
George R. Wilson

1990s
Jaconna Aguirre
Amy Kennedy*
Ty Russell
Hugh Scott

Mike Simons**
Bryan Terry

2000
Nate Billings
Michael Downes*
Chieko Hara**
Emily Schwarze**
Bill Waugh

* Part time
** College intern

NEWSPAPER AND WEB SITES
THE DAILY OKLAHOMAN   OKLAHOMA CITY TIMES   SUNDAY OKLAHOMAN   SATURDAY OKLAHOMAN AND TIMES   THE OKLAHOMAN   NEWSOK.COM